102.85

What Am I Doing With My Life?

What Am I Doing With My Life?

Late night internet searches
answered by the great
philosophers

Stephen Law

RIDER
LONDON • SYDNEY • AUCKLAND • JOHANNESBURG

1 3 5 7 9 10 8 6 4 2

Rider, an imprint of Ebury Publishing,
20 Vauxhall Bridge Road,
London SW1V 2SA

Rider is part of the Penguin Random House group of companies
whose addresses can be found at global.penguinrandomhouse.com

First published by Rider in 2019
www.penguin.co.uk

A CIP catalogue record for this book is available from the
British Library

ISBN 9781846046186

Typeset in 11/18 pt Camphor Std
by Integra Software Services Pvt. Ltd, Pondicherry

Printed and bound in Great Britain by Clays Ltd, Elcograf S.p.A.

Penguin Random House is committed to a sustainable future
for our business, our readers and our planet. This book is
made from Forest Stewardship Council® certified paper

Contents

Contents

Introduction

There was a time when, after a hard day's harvest-gathering, hunting, or weaving, we would gaze up at the heavens and soberly ask ourselves a few searching questions. We would ask about the meaning of life, and whether there is more to life than this. We would ask ourselves whether we were good or bad people. We would wonder why good people suffer. And we would agonise about whether we'd made the right decision.

Nowadays, late at night, after a hard day's work in the office, we're rather more likely to be on the internet, Googling. And yet, interestingly, we're still asking many of the same questions.

The autocomplete answers offered by internet search engines are a good indicator of the kind of questions people are typing in. Put 'What am I do ...' into Google and the first suggestion is 'What am I doing with my life?' Other autocomplete questions include: 'Is there more to life than this?', 'Am I a good person?', 'Does my life have meaning?', 'Why do good people suffer?', and 'Am I going to hell?'

This is a book of such questions. Most are actual autocomplete questions provided by Google. All of them are the kind of take-a-step-back questions we tend to ask when we have a little time on our hands to reflect and take stock.

Some of the questions are pretty obviously philosophical. They're the same questions that the so-called 'Great Philosophers' such as Socrates, Aristotle, and Kant pondered. Even when the questions are not obviously philosophical, it turns out that philosophy can often provide some useful insight. Sometimes a little philosophical clarification can help clarify exactly what it is we're asking. Sometimes knowledge of one or two philosophical arguments or concepts can help us make some real progress in providing answers to our questions.

In a way, this is a 'self-help' book. It's a book that shows how philosophy – including, in many cases, philosophical ideas and insights from the Greats – can help us figure things out for ourselves. It's not a book that just drops the answers into your lap so that you won't have to think about the questions anymore. You'll need to apply your own intellectual and emotional intelligence to figure out the answers, but my hope is that, having read this book, you'll be much better equipped to do that. It's a book that aims to help you *think better*, by providing many of the philosophical insights, thinking tools, and useful distinctions that you would pick up on a good introductory undergraduate philosophy course. I hope you will discover that, far from being irrelevant to everyday life, a little experience of philosophy is extraordinarily useful when tackling the often serious and important questions that almost all of us ask ourselves from time to time.

Sometimes I attempt to supply an answer (though don't just accept it on my say-so: make up your own mind). Other times you'll see that I'm not sure about the answer. Quite often I do no more than provide a few pointers that I hope you will find useful. You can dip into the questions in any order that suits you – as if you were Googling them yourself.

Stephen Law,
Oxford

▷ Result

Most of us want friends. While a few prefer solitude and a hermit-like existence most of us value friendship greatly. Some value it above almost everything else. The Ancient Greek philosopher Aristotle (384–322 BC) insists a life without friends isn't worth living. Friendship, he says, is 'most necessary with a view to living … for without friends no one would choose to live, though he had all the other goods'. Another Ancient Greek, Epicurus (341–270 BC), maintains that friendship is essential for happiness: 'Of all the things that wisdom provides to help one live one's entire life in happiness, the greatest by far is the possession of friendship.'

Supposing we lack friends, why is that, and what can we do about it?

Once you start wondering *why* you don't have any friends, various thoughts may pop into your head. One

1

obvious thought is: 'Do I lack friends because I am *unlikeable*?' But actually, plenty of rather unlikeable, indeed pretty awful, people seem to have close friends.

One sort of dislikeable person – the gossip who enjoys finding fault in others – can even be at an advantage when it comes to making friends. It's claimed that Alice Roosevelt Longworth (President Teddy Roosevelt's daughter) had a pillow embroidered with the motto: 'If you can't say something good about someone, sit right here by me.' Social psychologists confirm that sharing negative attitudes towards others helps bring people closer together.[1]

Certainly, the tightest teenage friendship groups are often some of the most gossipy. Those on the inside may feel more tightly bound together if they are unpleasant towards, and ostracise, those outside. In short, it seems that being obnoxious is no obstacle to having friends.

Probably the most obvious explanation offered for why people don't have any friends is that they're not putting themselves 'out there'. If we are not placing ourselves into situations where friends can be made, then a lack of friends is more or less guaranteed. Still, even if we have a healthy social network and full social calendar, we might still feel that we lack *true* friends. Real friendship, we may feel, involves more than just having people we see on a regular basis – at clubs, parties, and other gatherings. If that's our concern, if we find ourselves feeling lonely even in a room filled with other people, then perhaps we need to think about what real friendship involves.

Aristotle points to three different kinds of friendship, two of which are common, and one much more profound.

Some friendships, thought Aristotle, are based on their *usefulness* to us. They provide tangible economic, political or other advantages to us. For example, we may strike up friendships with people at work who can help us with our careers. Friendships based on their usefulness aren't necessarily exploitative. The advantages gained can be reciprocal: I'll scratch your back and you scratch mine.

A second sort of friendship, thought Aristotle, is focused on *pleasure*: I may make friends with people who I find amusing, for example, or with whom I can play sport, or go drinking or to concerts, which I enjoy.

Aristotle suggests these first two forms of friendship are likely to be comparatively short-lived. Friendships based on pleasure are dependent on what we find pleasurable, and that may well change – particularly when we're young. If I become less interested in sport, and more in playing cards, my circle of friends will probably shift accordingly.

Aristotle contrasts these first two forms of friendship with a third, deeper form of friendship. In friendships of this more profound sort, we don't love the other person because they help us obtain something we want. Rather, we love them because of *the sort of person they are*. We love them because we – being of good character – recognise *their* good character. And because good character endures, thinks Aristotle, so do such friendships:

> Now those who wish well to their friends for their sake are most truly friends; for they do this by reason of their own nature and not incidentally; therefore their friendship lasts as long as they are good – and goodness is an enduring thing.[2]

Of course, Aristotle is not suggesting such friendships can't be enjoyable or useful: they can. Though they may not *aim* at pleasure, they are pleasurable. They can be useful too. He suggests that a friend of this third sort holds up a mirror to you, providing an honest, warts-and-all reflection, thereby helping you become a better person.

If this last kind of friendship is what you are really after, then you need to be, or become, a good person, and to seek out other good people. Going out of your way to help others – perhaps by working as a volunteer – would be a good place to start. The advice may be clichéd, but it's also pretty sound: if you want to make friends, you really do need to 'put yourself out there'.

▶ Result

In 2004, a piece of toast was sold for $28,000.

The toast is supposed to show the face of the Virgin Mary.

Some really believe the toast was miraculous. In fact, every year all sorts of extraordinary appearances are reported: Mother Teresa appearing on a bun, Jesus appearing on the back of a bedroom door, and even on the back of a horseshoe crab shell. What's the explanation for these astonishing manifestations?

All these supposedly miraculous appearances are examples of a more general phenomenon called *pareidolia*. *Pareidolia* involves the mind perceiving a pattern in vague, randomly produced, shapes and sounds. That we're particularly prone to see faces and other people in the output of mere chance has been known for centuries. The Scottish philosopher David Hume (1711–1776) notes: 'There is a universal tendency among mankind to conceive all beings like themselves ... We find human faces in the Moon, armies in the clouds.'[3]

Perhaps the best-known example of pareidolia involves the planet Mars. In 2001, NASA's Viking 1 Orbiter spacecraft was circling Mars, taking photographs of the surface. As it passed over the Cydonia region, it took a photograph of what appeared to be an enormous, reptilian-looking face 800 feet high and nearly two miles long.

NASA revealed the image, saying it was a 'huge rock formation ... which resembles a human head ... formed by shadows giving the illusion of eyes, nose and mouth'. However, others thought this 'Face on Mars' was evidence that there had been some sort of civilisation on Mars. They thought they could discern other artificial structures nearby, including pyramids, and concluded that this was the site of an Ancient Martian civilisation. The truth, however, was later revealed by photographs taken by other spacecraft which showed that the 'face' was just a hill that happened to look face-like when lit from a certain angle.

The Mars Face – as well as faces seen in fruit, cliffs, the embers of a fire or clouds – is a result of two things.

First, some of the random patterns thrown up in our environment will, by chance, look like faces. That's to be expected. Others will look like dogs, horses, or Jesus. Stare up at the clouds on a breezy day and you can watch a whole menagerie float by. Second, it seems we're particularly prone to see faces in randomly produced visual noise. One scientific study concluded: 'Our findings suggest that human face processing has a strong top-down component whereby sensory input with even the slightest suggestion of a face can result in the interpretation of a face.'[4]

As a result of these two factors combining, we humans can easily see faces where there are none: including in that famous piece of toast.

There are also auditory versions of pareidolia. Some believe that in the white noise produced by a detuned radio it's possible to hear the voices of the dead talking to us. Such 'electronic voice phenomena', which feature in various horror films, are another product of our natural tendency to 'detect' humans and other agents (dogs, aliens, ghosts, fairies or gods) where in truth there are none. This tendency is amplified by the power of suggestion: tell people there's a message to be heard in some random noise, or a record played backwards, and there's a good chance they'll 'hear' it.

So, what explains this tendency to over-detect faces and voices? One explanation, offered by Carl Sagan in his book *Demon Haunted World*, is that the tendency is a product of our evolutionary heritage. A baby that can recognise its parents' faces is more likely to win their hearts and prosper than a child that can't. Humans who can easily detect a human or animal face in the bushes are more likely to avoid or survive being attacked by a rival or eaten by a predator. We have evolved to over-detect faces because missing faces is likely significantly to reduce our chances of surviving and reproducing, while 'seeing' a face where there isn't one is unlikely to be so costly.

Whether or not the above explanation is correct, there's no doubt we are highly prone to seeing faces and hearing voices where in truth there are none. That piece of toast is just one example of this peculiar tendency.

3. Am I being manipulated?

If we want to shape the beliefs of others, how might we do that? One of the most obvious ways of getting someone to believe something is to give them a good supporting *argument* for it.

Sometimes the arguments we offer are based on *evidence*. If I want you to believe the Earth is round and that dinosaurs once roamed the Earth, I can point to the overwhelming evidence supporting these beliefs, such as the way objects disappear over the horizon or the fossil record.

Other times, we can show that a belief is true by engaging in some *mathematical calculation* or *armchair reflection*. For example, by doing some calculations on the back of an envelope, I could show my friend that if their bathroom floor measures 12 feet by 12 feet, then they'll need at least 144 one-foot square tiles to cover it.

Yet another way I might get someone to believe that, say, there's an orange on the table is just to *show them* directly that the belief is true. If I point and say, 'Look, there is an orange!' and they then look and see it, they'll almost certainly come to believe an orange is there.

So, we can influence what others believe by providing them with good reasons and arguments, and also just by directly showing them that something is true. But these aren't the only ways we can influence what others believe. Many other mechanisms are available. Here are six.

First, we can apply *reward and punishment*. A kindly grandmother might try to influence the beliefs of her grandson by smiling approvingly when he expresses the 'right' beliefs and frowning when he expresses the 'wrong' beliefs. Reward and punishment can also be brutal. Under a totalitarian regime, those who dissent might be tortured and killed.

Secondly, we can employ *emotional manipulation*. For example, advertisers, cults, religions, and political parties all tend to associate very positive, uplifting imagery with the beliefs they want you to hold, and disturbing and frightening imagery with the beliefs they want you to reject.

Repetition is also useful. In some places, young people are encouraged to repeat certain stock phrases and sing songs of conviction each morning – praising their leader, their party, their political system or their country. Cults encourage mantra-like repetition of the tenets of their faith. Repeat a claim often enough, and belief may eventually take root.

Censorship and control of information can also be used to influence belief. If you don't want people to hold certain beliefs, then ensure they never hear about them. By removing books from libraries, censoring newspapers, and preventing dissenters from speaking, it's possible to restrict the range of beliefs people are likely to hold.

Isolation and peer pressure are also powerful mechanisms for shaping belief. Cults typically try to isolate new recruits, removing them from their old circle of friends and family and surrounding them with a new peer group of True Believers. Peer pressure can play a very significant role in influencing belief. Disagreeing with friends and family, especially when it comes to politics and religion, can be an uncomfortable experience.

A sixth tool at your disposal is to exploit the fact that humans find *uncertainty* uncomfortable, particularly when it comes to the big themes of love, sex, death, and doing the right thing. We fret when we're not sure what we should do. That discomfort is often exploited by cults and political regimes. They often offer recipes for living and believing reassuringly packaged as cast-iron certainties. They warn that if you step outside their charmed circle of certainty you will fall into chaos and darkness.

To some extent, we all influence the beliefs of others using these six mechanisms. For example, parents habitually make use of these mechanisms in trying to shape the beliefs of their children. They seek out the 'right' peer groups for their kids and put obstacles in the way of them befriending youngsters with the 'wrong' beliefs. Some parents might encourage repetition of the Pledge of Allegiance, the Scout Promise, or the Lord's Prayer, for example. They often offer their children inducements not just to behave in certain ways, but also to believe in certain things: God, or the American Dream, or equal rights, or democracy, or whatever it might be. The advertising industry also relies on these mechanisms to shape our beliefs about what we should buy. Adverts are usually emotionally manipulative, typically repeated, offer various inducements, and are highly selective in the information they provide.

So, when are we guilty of manipulating others? My suggestion is that, to the extent that we are relying very heavily on these six mechanisms – rather than on reason – to shape the beliefs of others, we're manipulating them. Here's an interesting fact about these mechanisms: *they work just as effectively whether the beliefs you are trying to instil are true or false.* Censorship and control, emotional manipulation, repetition, and so on, are just as effective whether you are trying to get people to believe that the Moon is made of rock and dust or that the Moon is made of cheese. Regimes and religions have used these mechanisms to convince people of countless falsehoods.

The attractive thing about appealing to someone's power of reason, on the other hand, is that *it strongly favours the truth*. Try to construct a sound, scientifically well-supported argument for supposing that the Moon is made of cheese or that there are fairies at the bottom of your garden. You won't find it easy, precisely because these claims aren't true. Of course, there's no cast-iron guarantee that if you apply reason, you'll end up believing what's true. But you have a much better chance of believing the truth if you subject claims to rational scrutiny.

Unlike the six techniques we examined above, reason doesn't favour the beliefs of the 'teacher' over those of the 'pupil'. Rather, it just favours the truth. So, if you use reason to persuade, you run the risk that your pupil may use reason to show that *you* are the one who's mistaken. That is a risk that some so-called 'educators' would prefer not to take.

Heavy reliance on these six mechanisms to the exclusion of rational argument is a bad thing. It makes our beliefs sensitive, not to the truth, *but to the whim of those employing them*. It can even amount to brainwashing.

According to Kathleen Taylor, neuroscientist and author of *Brainwashing: The Science of Thought Control*:

> One striking fact about brainwashing is its consistency. Whether the context is a prisoner of war camp, a cult's headquarters or a radical mosque, five core techniques keep cropping up: isolation, control, uncertainty, repetition and emotional manipulation.[5]

If we want to avoid being manipulated, we need to be able to spot when these techniques are being used on us. Unfortunately, that isn't easy. Emotional manipulation and peer pressure can easily cast their spell over us without our being aware. I might *think* I believe in equal rights because I recognise the rational force of the arguments for it. However, maybe I've just succumbed to a combination of repetition, emotional manipulation, and peer pressure? Certainly, if I told my highly liberal friends and family that men have more rights than women, I'd get frowns and might find myself cold-shouldered.

So, why do I believe what I do? And why do you? Just how rational are we? Perhaps we're more like the cultists than we'd like to think.

Q **4. Are ghosts real?**

 Result

<u>A ghost is usually thought of as the soul or spirit</u> of a dead person or animal that can appear to the living. Belief in ghosts is widespread. A 2013 poll found that 57 per cent of US citizens believe in ghosts. TV programmes on ghost hunting are highly popular.[6]

Sometimes ghosts are 'seen'. Other times their presence is supposed to be revealed by knockings, bangings, disembodied voices, strange cold spots and odours, and by objects apparently moving by themselves. And technology is now also being used in ghost hunting. Enthusiasts now use Electromagnetic Field (EMF) detectors, infrared cameras, highly sensitive microphones, and other devices to try to reveal the presence of the dead among us.

Belief in ghosts has a long history. The Ancient Greek philosopher Plato (c.428/427 or 424/423–348/347 BC) believed in ghosts. He believed that we are each an immortal, immaterial being. When we die, our immortal souls *should* return to the immaterial, invisible realm to which they belong and where they can be happy (see 'Is there more to life than this?' on page 243). However, if we've become overly fond of our physical bodies and the physical pleasures they allow, we may linger and become visible ourselves. Plato says such a soul:

> has become heavy and is dragged back to the visible region in fear of the unseen and of Hades. It wanders, we are told, around graves and monuments, where shadowy phantoms, images that such souls produce, have been seen, souls that have not been freed and purified but share in the visible, and are therefore seen.[7]

Not all ghosts are thought to be human. The Black Drummer Inn on St Ebbe's Street in my hometown of Oxford was supposedly haunted by a pig that squealed and oinked, and also destroyed bags and bit the feet of those who entered its room. The animal's spirit was allegedly eventually driven out when a local 'wise man' removed a 'corpse' from the building and destroyed it.

So, do the dead walk among us? The evidence that they do is not particularly strong. Despite decades of searching, armed with cameras, recording devices, and particularly if we already believe in spooky stuff. In one experiment, subjects who were told they were in a séance were much more likely to believe the false suggestion of the 'psychic' that the table had moved, when it hadn't, if they already believed in the paranormal. And around a fifth of all the subjects involved in the experiment thought they had witnessed real paranormal activity, when in truth nothing had happened: it was merely *suggested to them* that objects had moved by themselves. If these witnesses had not been told the truth when the experiment had finished, no doubt many would have later told people they had witnessed genuine paranormal activity, despite the fact that *nothing had actually happened*. Such is the power of suggestion.[8]

A third reason why we're likely to hear supposedly true tales of ghosts, even if ghosts don't exist, is that some people deliberately fake the evidence. Back in the 1840s, famed spiritualists the Fox sisters wooed large audiences with public séances in which they supposedly communicated with the spirits of the dead. The deceased would answer questions by making knocking and rapping noises. Later, Margaret, one of the sisters, confessed to faking messages from the departed by making the noises with her toes and legs. Even when there's no deliberate fraud involved, we can still inadvertently create or embellish ghostly tales, sometimes by leaving out key details. In one episode of a TV ghost hunting programme, a 'sneeze' was heard and recorded in a dark basement. Later, investigators discovered the real cause of the 'sneeze' was an automatic, motion-sensitive air freshener, not a ghost. That last fact was left out of the final, broadcast programme, resulting in a much more exciting episode.

Obviously, to point out that the evidence for ghosts is not strong is not to establish that ghosts *aren't* real, or that no one has ever seen a real ghost. Perhaps they have. But, given that most of the evidence we have for ghosts is based on testimony and experiences of the sort we should expect *anyway*, whether or not ghosts are real, it's wise to be pretty sceptical.

5. Am I normal?

When people ask, 'Am I normal?' they're often looking for reassurance. What they mean is: Am I normal, or do I have some sort of *problem* that needs addressing? For example, they may ask: Is it normal to feel this miserable, to struggle as much as I do to spell correctly, to be as interested – or disinterested – in sex as I am, or to have hair sprouting *there*?

It can be reassuring to hear that you're normal – that you're not freakish. However, that you're *not* normal is sometimes precisely what you *do* want to hear. You'd much prefer to learn that you have some sort of medical, learning or other condition that explains the difficulties you're having. For example, for someone who has been struggling with reading and writing, discovering that the difficulties they're having are *not* normal, and that they have dyslexia, can be a huge relief.

21

We even fantasise about not being 'normal', especially as teenagers. True, we wish outwardly to *appear* 'normal' so we can fit in and not be picked on or bullied. That's especially true when we're at school. Yet at the same time we often fantasise about *not* being normal: of having superpowers, or about being vampires, werewolves or secret royalty.

But what, precisely, does 'normal' mean?

Mostly, we use words unthinkingly. We entertain no doubts about what we, or others, mean by them. Yet, once we ask: 'But what *does* this word mean, *precisely*?' we can quickly get out of our philosophical depth. Asking the question about 'normal' is a good example. Here are a few attempts to pin down exactly what the word means and some of the difficulties we can encounter.

One obvious suggestion is that to say someone is normal is to say they are fairly average, or like most people. And it's certainly true that things that are common or average are often also deemed normal. For example, the normal body temperature for a human being is the temperature most human beings have, on average: 36.9°C (98.4°F). A normal IQ is an IQ that doesn't differ markedly from the average.

However, aren't there obvious counter examples to this definition of 'normal'? Take having red hair. Surely that's perfectly normal – and indeed natural – for humans. Yet it's also fairly unusual. Less than 2 per cent of us humans have red hair.

Often, when someone asks, 'Is this normal?', we need to ask: *'For what?'* Take having a neck as long as your legs. Is that normal? Yes, for a giraffe, it's normal. But for a mammal? Perhaps not, despite the fact that giraffes are mammals. Is having red hair normal? For a Scot? Certainly. For a human? Very probably. For someone of Chinese heritage? Perhaps not. Even when the relevant group has been specified, there can still be considerable disagreement about where normal ends. Am I normal if I'm in a minority of 10 per cent? Of 1 per cent? Of 0.01 per cent? Perhaps our definition of normal, in terms of not differing markedly from the average or majority, is correct. It's just that being in a minority of 2 per cent is not unusual *enough*.

Another way of dealing with the red hair example would be to switch to a different definition. It seems we also use 'normal' to mean something like 'naturally occurring' or 'what comes naturally'. At the hairdresser you might be asked 'Is that your *normal* hair colour?' The hairdresser might mean: is that your *usual* hair colour, the colour your hair is *most of the time* (dyed or not)? However, the hairdresser might instead mean: is that your *natural* hair colour (or is it dyed?). Having red hair, while pretty unusual for humans, is a natural human hair colour, unlike bright purple, which is artificial. So if normal is defined as *naturally occurring*, then red hair is normal for humans, despite being unusual.

'Normal' is used in other ways too. Sometimes it's used to mean something like: how things *should* be. Take two-headed calves, for example. Such calves, we may say, are 'not normal'. And by this we may mean not just that such calves are unusual – though they are – but that this is not how calves are *supposed to be* according to some sort of design plan. (Of course I use the term 'design plan' loosely: I don't mean that some intelligent being designed things that way). A two-headed calf involves a malformation: it has failed to develop in the way it is supposed to. Even if two-headed calves were rather more common – if they constituted 2 per cent of all calves, say – I suspect many of us would still say they weren't 'normal'.

Notice that a two-headed calf is something that occurs naturally every now and then. So such calves *are* normal in our second sense: they occur naturally, just like red hair in humans. Yet they aren't normal in our third sense.

Also notice, by the way, that being the way we're *meant* to be, according to some sort of design plan, isn't necessarily a good thing, and deviating from it isn't necessarily a bad thing. Suppose it turns out that humans have, as a result of their evolutionary history, evolved to be highly selfish and violent. Being selfish and violent is in our human design plan, just as being one-headed is in the calf design plan. But then to raise humans to be generous and peaceful would be to thwart that plan. Yet raising humans to be generous and peaceful might be a very good thing!

So let's now return to the question: 'Am I normal?' Someone asking this question may be asking: Am I, *statistically speaking*, normal for, say, a human? Or they may be asking: Is the way I am *natural*? Or they may be asking: Is this the way I'm *supposed to be* according to some sort of design plan (be it nature's plan or, if they believe in God, God's plan)? We may get different answers depending on which question we ask.

So here, at least, is an illustration of how philosophy can be of at least some practical help. It can help us get clearer about what question we're really asking. As the English philosopher John Locke (1632–1704) notes, a great deal of controversy results from people using the same term but with different meanings:

> Let us look into the books of controversy of any kind; there we shall see, that the effect of obscure, unsteady, or equivocal terms is nothing but noise and wrangling about sounds, without convincing or bettering a man's understanding. For if the idea be not agreed on betwixt the speaker and hearer, for which the words stand, the argument is not about things, but names.[9]

Certainly, on closer examination, controversies over what's normal often turn out to be a consequence of people using 'normal' in different ways.

6. Am I going to hell?

▶ Result

Every now and then I receive an email that promises me good fortune if I forward it to ten friends, and bad luck if I don't. These emails usually include stories about the horrific fate of those who failed to pass it on. Though I immediately send these emails to the trash, I appreciate why they are effective at getting themselves passed on. Even if you're fairly sceptical about the carrot and stick they waved at you, you might think that, still, it's a pretty scary stick, and ignoring it is a gamble not worth taking. Who wants to risk being cursed with bad luck?

Traditional Christianity offers an infinitely more impressive carrot and stick. Sincerely believe in Christ and you'll receive eternal life. Fail to do so and you will receive eternal damnation.

Hell, as traditionally understood, is very unpleasant indeed. St Augustine of Hippo (AD 354–430), having closely

27

examined various New Testament texts, concludes that hell is *literally* a lake of fire in which the damned will experience everlasting torment. If you're wondering how you can suffer being literally burned alive in a lake of fire without your body turning to a frazzle, Augustine explains that God miraculously keeps your body intact so that you can continue to suffer:

> … by a miracle of their most omnipotent Creator, [the damned] can burn without being consumed, and suffer without dying.[10]

Not all Christian thinkers understand hell in quite such physical terms. Some interpret hell as an absence of God. While not denying that hell is the worst possible thing we can experience, some think of its torments as being more psychological than physical. Other religions also posit a place of punishment beyond the grave. In Islam, it is called *Jahannam*, though Muslim scholars disagree about whether evil doers are sent there permanently.

So are *you* going to hell? And if so, why?

The traditional Christian view is that the hell-bound are those who *fail to believe*. If you die having failed to come to believe in God and – if you've heard about it – in the salvation Jesus offers, then you're damned. Religious belief is the only ticket out of hell.

Heaven and hell offer pretty extraordinary inducements to belief. There is literally no greater reward and no greater punishment conceivable.

Of course, belief in heaven and hell is closely associated with belief in God, and for an obvious reason. If you believe in God, then you believe in a supremely just and loving deity. But surely such a God won't tolerate a situation in which the torturer and murderer of a child never receives just punishment, and in which the child is gone forever, never to be compensated for the appalling wrong done to him or her? So, if you believe in God, believing in an afterlife in which these injustices are rectified is almost unavoidable. Hell may be awful, but it's just and indeed good that it exists, according to Christian philosopher William Lane Craig:

> For on the Christian view, hell is in fact good and the suffering of the damned just. The doctrine of hell constitutes the ultimate triumph of God's justice over evil; it assures us that we do, after all, live in a moral universe in which justice will prevail.[11]

On the other hand, the idea of hell strikes even many Christians as unjust, which is perhaps why opinion polls indicate that significantly more US citizens believe in heaven than hell.

Here's an obvious worry about the justice of hell. How can *infinite* punishment – endless, unbearable torment – *ever* be an appropriate penalty for our sins? Surely punishment should be proportionate and fit the crime?

Yet the sins we commit in a lifetime are always limited. No matter how much we've sinned, we could always have sinned more. But then why is infinite punishment ever deserved?

St Anselm (1033–1109) agrees that divine justice should be proportionate: 'God demands satisfaction in proportion to the extent of the sin.'[12] However, Anselm thinks our sins *are* infinite. In disobeying God, we disobey a being of infinite greatness. We therefore commit a sin of infinite magnitude. Any disobedience towards God, no matter how slight, even if it's just eating something God commanded us not to eat, merits the infinite punishment of hell.

This might sound ridiculous. What about infants who die before they have had a chance to disobey God? Do they deserve hell? And what about those who, due to cognitive impairment, have no grasp of the concept of God or of right and wrong? They can't have deliberately disobeyed God. So why do they deserve hell?

According to Augustine, they do. All humans are born sinners. Adam and Eve disobeyed God and we have inherited their original sin. Thus, even if we commit no sin in *this* life, we still deserve hell.

Perhaps one of the most disturbing questions about heaven and hell is: How can the good rest content in heaven when they know their loved ones are suffering unbearably for eternity? Actually, some theologians think that knowing – and indeed watching – the damned suffer is one of the joys of heaven. The American Protestant preacher and philosopher Jonathan Edwards (1703–1758) writes:

> When the saints in glory … shall see how miserable others of their fellow-creatures are, who were naturally in the same circumstances with themselves; when they shall see the smoke of their torment, and the raging of the flames of their burning, and hear their dolorous shrieks and cries, and consider that they [the saints] in the meantime are in the most blissful state and shall surely be in it to all eternity; how will they rejoice![13]

But surely no parent can be blissful in heaven knowing their child will forever experience the agony of hell? So does God perhaps remove all memory of that parent's loved ones? Does God make them blissfully *ignorant* about the torture of their offspring? But making us ignorant doesn't sound very God-like.

While the idea of cosmic justice is appealing, it's not clear that heaven and hell, as traditionally conceived, really deliver it. In fact, heaven and hell strike many of us – myself included – as terrifically *un*just. Surely no just and loving God would send you there for failing to believe in him?

7. Why have children?

▶ Result

People give many reasons for wanting to have children. Some reasons are entirely selfless: we want to bring new human life into the world, with all of the opportunities for happiness and achievement that brings. Watch some children playing happily in a park and you might well think, 'Who *wouldn't* want to create more of this?' We think of humanity as being a good thing, and humanity can only continue if we reproduce. So: having children is a good thing!

Of course, some also have selfish reasons for having children. Some feel their own lives won't be complete unless they procreate. And some have offspring with an eye to their own twilight years. Children and grandchildren can provide us with both company and security in our old age.

Still, while almost everyone thinks having children is a good thing, *is* it a good thing? You can be confident that when almost everyone assumes something is true, a philosopher will come along and question it, and perhaps make a persuasive-looking case for supposing it *isn't* true.

The German philosopher Arthur Schopenhauer (1788–1860) thought human existence more of a burden than a blessing. He concluded that it was irrational to procreate:

> If children were brought into the world by an act of pure reason alone, would the human race continue to exist? Would not a man rather have so much sympathy with the coming generation as to spare it the burden of existence, or at any rate not take it upon himself to impose that burden upon it in cold blood?[14]

However, this 'antinatalist' view – the view that we ought not to have children – is much older than Schopenhauer. You can even find the view that it would be better never to have been born expressed in the Old Testament:

> And I declared that the dead, who had already died, are happier than the living, who are still alive. But better than both is the one who has never been born, who has not seen the evil that is done under the sun.[15]

In response to Schopenhauer's suggestion that life is far more of a burden than a blessing, we might point to how the quality of human life has, in fact, improved markedly in many parts of the world, certainly since biblical times. One of the things we fear most about life is suffering. Yet, as mentioned earlier, we are learning to control our suffering. These improvements will no doubt continue. So what Schopenhauer calls the 'burden of existence' is getting smaller all the time.

South African philosopher David Benatar rejects this optimistic view. In his book *Better Never to Have Been*, he argues that coming into existence is *always* a serious harm, and that it's *always* wrong to have children. He's not proposing that people should be compelled not to have children but thinks it would be better if we didn't. However, Benatar acknowledges that, because of our deep biological urge to have children, few are going to agree with him.

According to Benatar, while human existence isn't pure suffering, it's sufficiently bad that we should avoid making more of it. He argues that there's *always more bad than good*. The worst pains, for example, are worse than the greatest pleasures. 'If you doubt this,' says Benatar, 'ask yourself – honestly – whether you would accept a minute of the worst tortures in exchange for a minute or two of the greatest delights.'[16] Pain also tends to be much longer lasting than pleasure. A sexual thrill or a delicious meal is a short-lived pleasure, whereas pain can last for months, years, or even a lifetime. Benatar also points out that ultimately we're never satisfied. When we get to eat regularly, for example, we naturally then start to focus on our next desire, and when that is satisfied, move on to yet another. Our lives are a ceaseless treadmill of striving, with no lasting contentment.

Most of us want to have children. For many, the urge is powerful, even overwhelming. However, just because we want to do it doesn't make it right. Like many philosophers, Benatar asks us some difficult and uncomfortable questions.

Q 8. Am I going to die? |

 Result

<u>Yes, of course you're going to die.</u> But is that a bad thing?

Most of us assume death is bad. It robs us of a future. It takes away our ability to pursue the things we care about and engage in activities we love. How could that not be a bad and indeed fearful thing?

Actually, not all philosophers agree that death is awful. The Ancient Greek philosopher Epicurus argues that death is not to be feared, no matter when it comes:

Why should I fear death?
If I am, then death is not.
If Death is, then I am not.
Why should I fear that which can only exist when I do not?[17]

Roman philosopher Lucretius (99–55 BC) agrees with Epicurus. It's not as if, when we are dead, we experience it. We're simply not there. And, Lucretius reminds us, we didn't exist for a long while *before* we were born. The universe existed without me in it for billions of years prior to my birth, and there is nothing fearful in that. So why should there being anything fearful in my absence later on?

Still, most of us won't be entirely reassured by that thought. Death does seem terrible, particularly for the young. Our desires – for a career, for children, to travel, and so on – are thwarted and whatever potential we had must now go unfulfilled. Surely those who die young really have been deprived of something valuable.

If it's a good idea to put off death, then there are things you can do to aid longevity, such as giving up smoking and eating healthily. As science develops, there will be yet more things you can do. Some believe we will eventually be able to *switch off the ageing process entirely*. Much of what we think of as ageing is a result of damage at the levels of the cells and molecules that accumulates in your body over the years. This damage could in principle be repaired. As technology and medicine develop, what we think of as the effects of old age may become entirely avoidable. We'll be able to carry on with the body of a contemporary twenty-year-old for as long as we wish – or at least until something other than ageing kills us. For, of course, we might still be run over by a bus, fall off a cliff or catch a fatal disease. Advanced anti-ageing technology won't deliver immortality, but it will have the consequence that, though the years may pass, we shan't grow 'old'.

Another way to avoid death would be to have your body frozen so that it can be reanimated later, once science has developed both the cure for whatever killed you and the ability to reanimate you. Cryonics, as this technology is called, turns on the thought that what makes you *you* is your physical constitution, and, in particular, *the make-up of your brain*. If your brain could be preserved well enough after your death, then you could be resurrected.

Living things that have been frozen solid can return to life. When I was a teenager, I stored some fishing maggots in the freezer. The maggots came out as a solid block, but when thawed they started wriggling again. If maggots can be frozen solid and yet return to life, why not humans? Unfortunately, humans are much more complex and freezing really does kill us. The damage to our bodies caused by freezing would need to be repaired if the cryonically preserved are to be resurrected.

But perhaps preserving the *physical* you is unnecessary? Some believe our identities can be *uploaded*. Just as we can upload a computer document onto a memory stick and then later download it onto a different computer without moving anything physical from one computer to the other, so, it's suggested, you could in principle be uploaded to a different physical body. If what makes you *you* is the way your brain and nervous system are configured, why couldn't we move you from one brain to another by uploading all the necessary information about your current brain and then downloading you again into a new brain? In fact, why not download you into an electronic brain inside a robot body? By uploading ourselves, we could achieve immortality as an 'electronic person'.

The possibility of achieving immortality through uploading is one of the aims of an organisation called the *2045 Initiative*. This leads, however, to another question: would it really be you that was uploaded, or merely a *copy* of you?

Suppose I'm about to die. Then I discover that my brain has been scanned and an electronic version of 'me' has been uploaded and downloaded again into a new body that will live on. That doesn't seem much of a consolation as far as I'm concerned. Surely the person that survives won't be *me*, but merely someone *just like* me. I'll still be dead. But if that's true, perhaps it really does need to be this *physical* person that is resurrected later, and not just an uploaded copy, if I'm to survive.

Assuming future generations could bring us back from the dead, *should* they? Should we bring back a first-century Chinese goat herder if we could? It might be an interesting encounter for us, but for the deceased goatherder it would likely be a bewildering, perhaps terrifying, experience. The life they knew would be long gone. They might find it impossible to adjust to our modern existence. There may be little obvious benefit either to the resurrectors, or to the resurrected, in bringing the long-dead back to life.

Still, such ethical questions are at this point largely academic. The fact is you and I are going to die, and that will be our lot. Cheating death isn't currently an option.

9. Why don't I enjoy life?

▶ Result

<u>Happiness is elusive. It's something we strive</u> hard to obtain, yet rarely seem to achieve. In fact, the harder we try to attain it, the more quickly it can seem to recede over the horizon.

Happiness can be particularly difficult to achieve if we're not sure what we're after. What *is* happiness, exactly?

One obvious way of thinking about happiness is in terms of our *subjective feelings*. Professor Lord Richard Layard, a leading researcher on happiness, defines it in terms of 'feeling good'. To want happiness is to want to feel good, and to go on feeling good.

But that's just one conception of happiness. According to Aristotle, true happiness, or *eudaimonia*, is not a subjective feeling *at all*. Rather it is a feature of 'a complete lifetime'. The happy person, says Aristotle in his *Nicomachean Ethics*, is the person who has lived a life of virtue and good character:

> The good of man is the active exercise of his faculties in conformity with excellence of virtue (...) [T]his activity must occupy a complete lifetime; for one swallow does not a spring make nor does one fine day; and similarly one or a brief period of happiness does not make a man supremely blessed and happy.[18]

To contemporary ears, Aristotle's way of thinking about happiness may sound strange. Most of us no longer link happiness and morality. In fact, unlike Aristotle, most of us now assume that even bad people can be happy.

True, many contemporary religious people still link happiness and morality. However, unlike Aristotle, they tend to think of happiness not as a *feature* of the moral life, but as a *consequence*. The good person won't necessarily be happy in *this* life. Their reward comes later: in heaven. Historically, many Christians have gone out of their way to suffer in this life, hoping to achieve happiness in the next. They've denied themselves pleasures and punished themselves. They've even mutilated themselves.

Some cynics assume that what motivates someone to act is always, without any exception, to increase their own happiness. According to the 'psychological egoist', the person who gives to charity doesn't deserve praise. The charitable are merely trying to make themselves feel good, by achieving a feeling of holier-than-thou superiority, say. No one ever gives selflessly. There's *always* an ulterior motive.

Actually, psychological egoism is implausible. Some people may give to charity to make themselves feel good. However, suppose there was a magic pill that, if you took it, would induce a powerful delusion: that you have given to charity *even though you haven't*. Given the option of really giving to charity or taking that pill and keeping your cash instead, which would you choose? The fact is, almost everyone would choose to give to charity, and not just feel like they have. But that makes no sense if psychological egoism is true. While helping others obviously can make us feel good, that's not usually the reason we do it.

Here's another reason to doubt that happiness – understood as 'feeling good' – is what's most important to us. Suppose a machine is built that can produce any subjective experience. Plug yourself in and it will simulate whatever you wish. You can experience what it's like to climb Mount Everest or walk on the Moon. Your wildest fantasies can be indulged, from listening to Beethoven play piano to engaging in erotic acts with your favourite celebrity. The experiences the machine generates are indistinguishable from experiences of the real thing.

You would probably be keen to at least try out this machine – I certainly would. But suppose you were offered the opportunity to live out your entire life in the virtual world it creates? Suppose you're offered the opportunity to immerse yourself so fully that you will no longer even be aware that what you were experiencing is not, in fact, real. Would you accept that offer?

I suspect almost no one would. Yes, we want to feel good. But some things are even more important to us. A life lived out entirely in a stage-managed, virtual world is a life lived without any true friends, without any real relationships, and lacking the types of genuine accomplishments many of us desire (such as *really* to climb Everest, say). Most of us want to lead lives that are *authentic*. Someone who has lived out their life within a fake reality might subjectively *feel* content and fulfilled. But were they to be told on their deathbed that everything they had experienced had been an illusion – that they had made no real friends, that no one had really cared about them, that their greatest accomplishments were a fraud – then they might well feel that theirs was a life sadly wasted (this is a point we shall revisit in 'Is honesty the best policy?').

Still, while 'feeling good' is not what's most important to us, it is very important. So how can we increase our happiness? There's growing evidence to suggest that the recipe for happiness – in the sense of feeling good –

is actually *fairly* simple. Here are seven increasingly well-supported recommendations for making yourself happier:

1. *Develop good relationships.* Close friends and family whom we trust provide us with a support network and have a marked effect on our levels of happiness. Note that it's not the *number* of friends we have, but the *quality* of those relationships. The effect on our happiness is even more marked if we are close friends with people who are themselves happy.

2. *A reasonable level of income is important.* It's hard to be happy when you are worrying about how to pay the bills. Research suggests our well being rises with increases in income up to about $75,000 p.a. (depending on the cost of living). However, beyond that level, further increases in income – even to lottery-winning levels – turn out to have little lasting effect on happiness.

3. *Stop and smell the roses.* Taking a moment to focus on the here and now – sometimes called mindfulness – can improve how we feel. So find a moment each day or two to watch the clouds drift by. When you're eating a meal, don't wolf it down, but focus closely on how everything tastes. Take a couple of minutes to focus only on your breathing.

4. *Be kind and generous.* Helping others is an effective way of improving how we feel. Comment positively on others, to help them feel good. Spending time volunteering and spending money on others also helps to make us happier.

5. *Spend your money not on acquiring more stuff – cars, watches, clothes, computers, etc. – but on new experiences.* The happiness we gain from our purchases is sadly short-lived. Travel and adventure, enjoying a wonderful meal with friends, attending an amazing concert, or celebrating an event with a party are much more efficient ways of spending to find happiness.

6. *Exercise.* Regular exercise is known to help improve our mood.

7. *Be grateful.* Focusing for a moment each day on what's good in your life – perhaps by making a note in a diary or mentioning it to friends and family – can help boost your happiness (for more on this, see 'Why don't I appreciate what I have?' on page 155).

10. Am I racist?

We're all familiar with those who say 'I'm not racist but … ' and then go on to say something racist. Could I, too, be a racist without realising it? Could I be guilty of unconscious bias?

Racism is a form of bigotry. It involves prejudice and unjust discrimination against others on the basis of race. It's an example of our broader tendency to draw boundaries based on perceived racial, religious, sexual and other differences, and to then discriminate in favour of those on our side of the boundary. We humans are tribal creatures prone to thinking in terms of 'ingroup' and 'outgroup'.

Unfortunately, a number of the 'great' philosophers were outnight racists. Immanuel Kant (1724–1804) believed that 'the race of the whites' was closest to perfection, David Hume suggested that all other people

49

were inferior to 'the whites'.[19] And white UK and US slave owners would often quote Aristotle, who argued that some people are 'natural slaves'.[20]

One way in which we might try to measure racial bias is to apply the Implicit Association test or IAT. The test is designed to pick up unconscious bias against minorities based on, for example, race, gender, and sexual orientation. The 'race' test, for example, asks you to sort black and white faces and positive and negative words as fast as possible by pressing a left or right button. You can take the test yourself here:

https://implicit.harvard.edu/implicit/selectatest.html

The thinking behind this exercise is that if people taking the test associate, say, black people with negative traits, then they'll find it easier to link black faces with negative words, and so will respond more quickly. And so our bias is revealed. While explicit, conscious racial bias has been falling for decades, it's suspected many still harbour an implicit racial bias. It's that unconscious bias that the 'race' IAT is designed to reveal. Most who take the online test do show at least *some* degree of bias.

In another disturbing test, people looking at an image of someone carrying an ambiguous object were more likely to mistake a mobile phone for a gun and 'shoot' the carrier if he was an outgroup male. Research also suggests we tend to be even more suspicious of outsiders *when we feel threatened* – such as at night, for example. It seems that racism is, at least in part, exacerbated by fear. People who feel cornered and vulnerable are more prone to it.

If we all exhibit some degree of racial bias, then it's misleading to present the issue of racism as a battle between the racists vs. the rest. That sort of thinking would obscure the fact that we're all susceptible to it, and it makes it more likely that some of us will sit on our laurels, unaware of our own racism. It also demonises and makes an 'outgroup' of people with whom we share the same negative traits, even if we don't exhibit them to the same extent.

The philosopher George Yancy, in his article 'Dear White America', ingeniously uses the fact that we're *all* guilty of prejudice – Yancy included – to disarm white readers convinced that they're not guilty of racism.

> What if I told you that I'm sexist? Well, I am. Yes. I said it and I mean just that … There are few men, I suspect, who would say that they are sexists, and even fewer would admit that their sexism actually oppresses women. Certainly not publicly, as I've just done.[21]

Yancy explains that he doesn't *want* to be sexist. It's just that despite his best efforts and intentions, he continues to perpetuate sexism. He has failed to challenge sexism when he's seen it, and he says he's 'often ambushed' by his own hidden sexism. But he refuses to lie to himself and others and insist that he's not sexist.

Yancy then suggests to his white readers that while they may have black friends and relatives, don't blame black people for everything, and don't use the 'N' word, that *doesn't mean they're not racist.* They are:

> As you reap comfort from being white, we suffer for being black and people of color. But your comfort is linked to our pain and suffering. Just as my comfort in being male is linked to the suffering of women, which makes me sexist, so, too, you are racist. That is the gift that I want you to accept, to embrace. It is a form of knowledge that is taboo. Imagine the impact that the acceptance of this gift might have on you and the world.[22]

If Yancy is right, for white people to accept that we *are* racist is a valuable first step in dealing with racism.

While humans may be constitutionally prone to prejudices, many of us also actively monitor ourselves for such bigotry and do our best to combat it. We're never going to be perfect, but we can do a great deal to ensure we don't make negative judgements about outgroup folk based on irrational prejudices.

If you want to stop other people being racist, I doubt you'll achieve much by screaming, 'Racist!' at them. You can enjoy a little righteous indignation while denouncing them, of course. But you're unlikely to actually improve the racist.

Of course, having a constructive conversation about race is more difficult than just firing off angry accusations. But it is worth the effort. In particular, one study suggests that, by having conversations that encourage people to remember when *they* were *themselves* victims of prejudice, we can start to reduce their prejudice towards others. It seems that getting people to empathise with those they're prejudiced against is the key. And it seems that's not so difficult to do.[23]

11. Do I have free will?

The Ancient Greeks worried about fate. The Fates, they thought, were three goddesses who wove the tapestry of our lives on their loom. Whatever you do, and whatever will befall you, is predestined by the way the Fates have already woven the thread of your life into the fabric of history. Try as you might to avoid your fate, you cannot. Indeed, your attempt to thwart fate might actually bring about what they have predestined.

A nice example of fate in action is provided by an Ancient Mesopotamian tale retold by Somerset Maugham in his short story 'An Appointment in Samarra'. A merchant sends his servant to the marketplace for provisions. The terrified servant returns, saying that he saw Death in the marketplace and she made a threatening gesture towards him. The servant borrows the merchant's horse and gallops off to Samarra, seventy-five miles away, to try to avoid his fate. When the merchant goes to the marketplace he also sees Death, and he asks her why she threatened his servant. Death replies: 'That was not a threatening gesture, it was only a start of surprise. I was astonished to see him in Baghdad, for I have an appointment with him tonight in Samarra.'

The poor servant is fated to die that evening, and there's nothing he can do about it. But is fatalism true – the view that, no matter what we do, our futures are predestined? Obviously not. The ludicrousness of fatalism is demonstrated by the person who, when told they should wear a seatbelt as it may well save their life in a car accident, refuses, saying, *'Que será, será.* What will be will be. There's nothing I can do to change what will happen.' Clearly, what we do *can* alter the future. Installing seatbelts has saved thousands from serious injury or death. Donning a parachute before jumping out of a plane will likely save your life.

Still, even if fatalism is false, perhaps there remains another, rather more serious, threat to your freedom to determine how your life goes.

Science reveals that the universe is governed by natural laws. These laws determine how everything unfolds. Given sufficient knowledge of the laws of nature and how things are physically at a given moment, we can in principle predict what will happen in an hour, a day, a year or a decade's time. As we humans are a part of the physical universe, we're subject to those same laws. So everything *we* do can *also* be predicted long before we do it. Presented with a fork in the road, you may think you're free to choose the left fork or the right. But it turns out that whichever choice you make was determined long ago by the laws of nature and the prior physical state of the universe. Like a struck ball rolling across a billiard table, you can't do other than what the laws dictate.

Of course, we *think* we're free. It seems to us that we can make free choices and act on them. But perhaps we're nature's puppets and free will is an illusion?

Certainly, science has established that many things that seem obvious aren't actually true. It *seems* like the Earth is stationary. Yet science has established it moves. Why shouldn't science have revealed that free will, like a stationary Earth, is also an illusion?

While fatalism is easily dispensed with, this science-based threat to free will looks more serious. We now face a famous, and thorny, philosophical dilemma. On the one hand it *seems* to us that we're free. On the other hand, we've been presented with an argument that seems to establish free will is an illusion. So, something has to give. But what? There is no philosophical or scientific consensus about that. Some philosophers and scientists believe free will is an illusion. Others disagree.

One popular way of defending the claim that we have free will is to insist you must be free because sometimes you choose tea for breakfast, and other times coffee. So there's no 'law of nature' that determines that you will always choose tea rather than coffee. But this defence involves a misunderstanding. Obviously there's no law of nature that says you will always choose tea rather than coffee. However, the fact that you choose tea some days and coffee others is explained by the fact that there are physical differences between you on the days you choose tea, and you on the days you choose coffee – differences of which you are unaware. Which choice you make is still determined by the fundamental laws of nature and that precise physical situation.

But must we accept that every physical event has a physical cause? Some defend free will by insisting their mind is *not part of the physical universe*. When they decide to reach for the tea rather than the coffee, their non-physical mind makes a free, undetermined choice. Then, somehow, their mind causes a physical chain of events that results in their arm reaching for the tea.

This theory that the mind is something that is non-physical – thus escaping physical determinism – but that can nevertheless cause physical things to happen is the view of French philosopher René Descartes (1596–1650). Descartes thought your immaterial mind affects what's going on in your body via the pineal gland in the brain. He supposed the pineal gland functions, in effect, as an aerial. It receives input from the non-physical mind and turns it into physical activity. It also lets the mind know what's going on in the body. So, from Descartes' point of view, *some* physical events have no physical cause: namely, the mind-caused events that take place in our pineal glands.

However, there's growing scientific evidence that our bodies aren't under the control of an immaterial mind. It turns out that the brain activity of someone about to make a conscious decision – to press a button with either their right or left hand, for example – reveals physical changes that can allow an observer to predict which hand the person will use *a full seven to ten seconds* before that conscious decision is made. If someone's conscious decision to use their left rather than their right hand was made by an immaterial mind, it wouldn't be possible to predict which hand they would use by looking at what was happening in their brains seven to ten seconds earlier.

Another way in which we might try to salvage free will is to appeal to quantum indeterminacy. This is not as complicated as it sounds. A majority of physicists now lean towards the view that what happens at the quantum level – the level of the very, *very* small – is not *entirely* physically determined. It appears the laws of nature don't fix exactly where a subatomic particle will land in certain experiments, but only approximately where it will land. But if there is some indeterminacy at the quantum level, might this not allow for free will?

Actually, it's unclear why quantum indeterminacy or randomness, by itself, would deliver free will. Random events are no more events over which we have control than are physically determined events. If some freak, random event in my brain causes a spasm, so that my arm shoot outs and punches you on the nose, that's not an example of my freely choosing to punch you.

Currently, it seems that if we want to defend free will against the threat posed by physical determinism, our best bet is to try to show that free will and determinism are *compatible*. Perhaps, when we unpack what 'acting freely' means, it will turn out that we can act freely even if everything we do is also physically determined. But is this strategy for reconciling the findings of science with free will going to work? The jury remains out.

12. Are psychics real?

Result

Many people consult psychics. Sometimes they consult them hoping for some insight into the future. Sometimes they use them hoping to communicate with the dead. Psychics are big business, raking in many millions each year, and even corporations are known to make use of them. Financial psychic Lisa Jones is reported to charge $750 per session to advise her business clients.[24]

Surely, if people are prepared to pay such large sums for psychic advice, there must be *something* to it?

Well, maybe. There's little doubt most psychics are honest. They genuinely believe they have psychic powers. But could their seemingly spooky and supernatural ability have a more mundane explanation?

If you visit a psychic, the conversation might go something like this:

PSYCHIC: I am getting a name beginning with 'G'. George … Graham … Gary …

CLIENT: Gary! My Uncle Gary died last year.

PSYCHIC [*pointing to chest*]: I'm sensing some trouble here.

CLIENT: You're right! Gary died of a heart attack.

PSYCHIC: Do you have a box of unsorted photographs in your house?

CLIENT: Yes!

PSYCHIC: It's important you and your husband sort those photographs out, Gary says.

CLIENT: Er, my husband is dead.

PSYCHIC: Yes, I know. But Gary says your husband will be with you in spirit when you sort the photographs. Does 'Bambi' mean anything to you?

CLIENT: The deer? Yes – I like Babycham. It's my favourite drink, and there is a baby deer on the label! How did you know?

Suppose that afterwards, this client tells her friends that the psychic knew that her Uncle Gary died last year of a heart attack. The client also claims the psychic knew about a box of photographs that need sorting, and was even aware that her favourite drink was Babycham. Her friends are likely to be highly impressed.

But just how impressive was the psychic? In fact, this fairly typical 'psychic' reading involves a well-known technique called *cold reading*. Cold reading involves creating the impression that you know various things about a person without actually knowing anything at all. It combines a number of techniques.

The first technique is to use *Barnum statements*. The showman P. T. Barnum used to say that his show had 'something for everyone'. Barnum statements similarly offer something for everyone: they're statements that actually apply to most or many people, despite the fact that we often think they're specific to us. Classic examples are:

'So-and-so died from trouble in his chest.'
'You have a box of unsorted photographs in your house.'
'You are sometimes insecure, especially with people you don't know very well.'
'At times you have serious doubts as to whether you have made the right decision or done the right thing.'

Most of us will agree with these statements. So it's no surprise that our psychic scored 'hits' with the first two.

A second common cold-reading technique is *shotgunning*. This is where a number of often ambiguous claims are made with the hope that at least one scores a 'hit'. For example, almost everyone knows someone whose name begins with 'g'. And almost everyone – especially older people – will know at least one George, Graham or Gary. In short, the psychic didn't know the client had an uncle called Gary. It was actually *the client* who supplied that information. Shotgunning works especially well with a large audience. Even if the psychic makes a quite specific claim – for example, 'Does someone here know of an accident involving a dark blue car driven by a middle-aged woman?' – there's still a good chance it will ring true for at least one person in the audience.

Third, the psychic can rely on the fact that clients tend to remember the 'hits' and forget the 'misses'. The psychic suggested two other names that rang no bells before he got to 'Gary'. Those misses were ignored by the client, who focused only on the much more memorable 'hit'. Notice too how the psychic neatly dodged round the fact that the client's husband is dead by saying the husband will be present spiritually, if not physically, when the photographs are sorted. What looked like the psychic's mistake – supposing client's husband was alive – was quickly airbrushed away.

The psychic also mentioned 'Bambi' but gave no detail at all. This word has all sorts of potential significance, especially for older clients familiar with the Disney film *Bambi*. The client might have known someone with that nickname, or have seen the film on a first date with her husband, or have been particularly fond if it, or ... well, there are no end of connections with 'Bambi' the client might make. In this case the client makes a connection to a deer, and then, somewhat tenuously, to a drink, and then assumes the psychic knew about her liking that drink. But of course it was *the client* who provided all this information. And if 'Bambi' had meant nothing to the client, well, the psychic could move quickly on and that particular 'miss' would soon be forgotten.

Finally, a self-styled psychic can gain quite a lot of information from a person by observation. In this case, he spotted the client's wedding ring, so knew she was married.

It's no coincidence that most psychic sessions are shot through with these kinds of questions and statements. And if a psychic is relying on shotgunning, Barnum statements, and other cold-reading techniques, then they're not demonstrating real psychic ability. The explanation for how they 'know' what they know is fairly mundane. None of this is to suggest that most psychics are deliberate frauds. They're not. Most genuinely believe they have psychic powers.

I once experienced someone convincing themselves they had miraculous mind-reading abilities. I was performing a simple mind-reading trick with some family members. The trick involves setting up what looks like a spontaneous game of guessing the colour of the next playing card. In fact, I prearranged with my accomplice that if the card was black, I would say, 'OK', and if it was red I'd say, 'Right.' The trick is *so* obvious that many people miss it. They think the accomplice can read my mind. On this occasion, I started testing someone at the table – someone not in on the trick. And, amazingly, they too found they could magically predict the colour of the card. They got more and more excited at their amazing 'psychic' ability, and were then hugely disappointed when I revealed that they weren't psychic after all: they had just unconsciously picked up on the code I was using. If someone can so easily convince themselves they're psychic when they're not, it's not surprising that others can convince themselves they're psychic without realising they're just using cold-reading techniques.

Still, a few psychics are deliberate frauds. Some combine cold reading with hot reading. Hot reading involves researching the client before the session takes place. A psychic might google their client. Some psychics may even share information about their clients with other psychics (if you tell one psychic something, other psychics might then miraculously know about it). A lot of clients are referred by friends who may have told the psychic various facts about them. Psychics sometimes also begin their shows by encouraging audience members to fill out a card before the show and dropping it into a box or bowl, giving information on who they are, where they are from, and who they want to hear from. Less scrupulous psychics then use this information to manipulate their audience: 'I am getting a message from Mike, who died in a fire. Does that mean anything to anyone here?' Unsurprisingly, when someone in the audience stands up saying that, yes, they *do* know of a Mike who died in a fire, the psychic will then miraculously know the audience member's name and where they come from. Some fake psychics, spiritualists, and miracle-workers have even used radio earpieces to receive this sort of information. Faith healer Peter Popoff, who was a hugely successful American televangelist is the 1980s, used to receive messages via an earpiece from his wife, Elizabeth, who read the information off cards submitted by the audience. He was caught when magician James Randi and his team took a radio scanner to one of Popoff's events.

The English philosopher C. D. Broad (1887–1971) was particularly interested in paranormal phenomena, because he thought that *if* they were genuine, then they had philosophically important consequences. For example, if people can foresee the future, then that suggests backwards causation occurs (meaning that what will happen in the future can have an effect now), which is something most of us assume is impossible. And if people can talk to the dead, then that suggests physicalism (the view that only the physical world exists) is false, for human beings can continue to exist independently of their physical, deceased bodies. In short, if it could be established that the paranormal was real, that would be philosophically revolutionary! Consequently, Broad thought it important to test in a rigorous, scientific way whether any genuine paranormal phenomena exist. Many experiments investigating the paranormal have since been done. To date, there's little, if any, credible scientific evidence that some people are genuinely psychic, though perhaps such evidence will yet turn up.

13. Can I 'just know' things?

 Result

Sometimes, when we're asked how we know something, we'll say, 'Look, I *just know*!' But what does that mean, exactly? Sometimes we just mean the person should take our word for it because we don't have time to set out all the evidence. But other times it seems we mean something else. Like in this example:

MARY: You're saying that your dead Uncle Albert comes and visits you every day?

JOHN: Yes, he does. He's in the room with me right now. I can *sense his presence.*

MARY: But maybe you're imagining it? What *evidence* have you got that Uncle Albert is visiting you from beyond the grave?

JOHN: I don't have or need *evidence. I just know*!

This is an example of someone claiming to 'just know' something despite their not possessing any good evidence or argument to support their belief.

John's belief about visits from beyond the grave is probably fairly harmless. Still, there are times when the belief that we 'just know' something can have serious consequences.

During the Iraq war, President George Bush often ignored the evidence provided by military and political experts. Bush chose instead to be guided by what he called his 'gut'. The President thought his gut was functioning as a sort of *God sense*, letting him know by 'instinct' what God wanted him to do. Bush thought he 'just knew' that God wanted him to go to war with Iraq. And the consequences of that were enormous.

People may claim to 'just know' things because they suppose they have some sort of spirit sense or God sense. Others claim to 'just know' things about the future through some sort of psychic sense. What, if anything, is wrong with such claims? Isn't it at least possible that some of us really do have such extraordinary senses?

The attitude of President George Bush would have horrified the mathematician and philosopher W. K. Clifford (1845–1879). Clifford claimed that:

… it is wrong, always and everywhere, to believe anything on insufficient evidence.[25]

But is that true? Actually, some philosophers believe that 'just knowing' without evidence – and perhaps even *contrary* to the available evidence – is a possibility.

One problem with Clifford's demand that beliefs always be supported by evidence is that, in order to justify your first belief – let's call it Belief A – you'll presumably need *to believe that that supporting evidence exists*. But then Clifford's principle requires that this *second* belief *in turn* requires evidence. And then you'll need to believe *that* supporting evidence exists, and so will need evidence for *that* belief, and so on.

You can now see that Clifford's demand that every belief be supported by evidence appears to generate an *infinite regress*. To be entitled to hold even one belief I'll need to justify an infinite number of beliefs. And that can't be done. The upshot, it seems, is that if Clifford is right, *it's wrong to believe anything at all*. Including the belief that Clifford is right! But that's ridiculous. So, many draw the conclusion that Clifford must be wrong.

It appears that if we're to be allowed to know anything at all, Clifford's requirement is going to have to be relaxed. There must be occasions on which we are entitled to believe despite lacking evidence.

In fact, some philosophers argue that we can know things without evidence. We can, as it were, 'just know'.

For example, according to one leading theory of knowledge known as *reliabilism*, in order to know that, say, there's an orange on the table in front of you, you just need *reliably functioning senses*. If your eyes are working properly, and you're in a situation where you can't easily go wrong in your beliefs by relying on your eyes, then, if you believe there's an orange on the table because that's how it looks to you, you can *know* there's an orange there. You don't need any *evidence* there's an orange there – at least not in the sense that you must *infer* that the orange is there on the basis of other things you know to be true. Just so long as there is an orange there and that belief is produced by reliably functioning senses, you can *know* there's an orange there.

But if that's true, then *if* some of us also have not only reliably functioning eyes, but also a reliably functioning God sense, or spirit sense, or psychic sense, then some of us could 'just know' that God wants us to invade another country, or that a dead relative is in the room with us. We wouldn't *need* evidence!

Not only could you potentially 'just know' what God wants you to do or that your dead uncle is in the room with you, you could perhaps *also reasonably believe* these things. We consider many beliefs reasonable given only that they *really seem* to be true. If I look out of the window and seem to see a bus there, then surely it's reasonable for me to believe there's a bus there, especially if I don't have any reason to suspect my eyes are somehow deceiving me.

In fact, couldn't I reasonably believe there was a bus there even if I had some strong evidence supporting the view that there's *no* bus there? Suppose, for example, that I had just heard it reported on a usually very reliable radio programme that no buses at all are out today because of a strike. Surely I could *still reasonably believe* there is a bus outside, despite my having that strong piece of evidence that there are no buses on the streets today?

So, generally speaking, *it's reasonable to believe that how things appear is how things are.* But then if it really seems to someone that God exists, or that their dead uncle is in the room with them, then it can be reasonable for them to believe those things too!

To sum up: there are philosophers who would allow that *in principle*, some people can *reasonably believe*, and also *know*, that God exists, that God wants them to start a war, or that their dead relatives are visiting, despite not having any evidence to support their belief. Actually, I'm pretty sympathetic to this view.

So do I believe that some of us *really do* have a reliable God sense, or a reliable spirit sense? No, I'm not convinced of that. I think such super-senses are, in principle, possible.

However, I think there's pretty good evidence that these extra senses don't actually exist.

Take, for example, the God sense. Many people claim to have experienced the divine by means of a God sense – or what the French theologian John Calvin (1509–1564) called a *sensus divinitatis*. However, there's considerable disagreement among them about what the divine is like. Some sense the presence of one God; others sense many gods. Some sense something terrifying, others something loving. Some, like George Bush, sense a deity that wanted the US to invade Iraq. Others sense a deity that insists that violence is never the answer. Some say God tells them money is a sign of divine favour. Others say God will not allow the rich to enter the Kingdom of Heaven. Some say God has revealed to them that Jesus is God. Others say God denies this. In short, our supposed God senses often *flatly contradict each other*. But then we can be sure that a fair percentage of the beliefs they deliver are false.

We also know that humans are highly prone to believing falsely that they're experiencing extraordinary hidden beings, such as ghosts, dead ancestors, spirits, sprites, elves, gnomes, fairies, angels, demons, and aliens. Many of these experiences have been debunked. For example, some have been pretty conclusively shown to be a product of illusion or the power of suggestion. So, given we're so prone to believing that we're experiencing extraordinary invisible beings when we're not, shouldn't we be pretty sceptical, not just about the beliefs of others based on such experiences, but also our own?

14. Does my life have meaning?

Sometimes, when we take a step back and look at our lives, we ask ourselves: 'What's the *meaning* of all this? Does my life have any meaning?'

This is an odd sort of question. Usually, if someone were to ask what's the meaning of a mushroom, or the sky, or blancmange, we'd scratch our heads in bafflement. 'What on Earth do you *mean*?' we might well say, 'blancmange doesn't *have* a meaning.'

Of course, it does make sense to ask for the meaning of a word, a book or a film, or something that symbolises something else. The *word* 'blancmange' has a meaning. It can also make sense to ask for the meaning of a red sky at night, if by that we mean: What does that red sky indicate? What is a red sky a *sign* of, weather-wise? But presumably, in asking, 'What's the meaning of my life, or human life in general?' we aren't supposing our lives,

77

like the word 'blancmange', are some sort of symbol or sign.

Actually, it's not that our lives *couldn't* have meaning in the sense of being used as a symbol or sign. Anything *can* have that sort of meaning. I might leave a mushroom in a flowerpot outside my door as a code to tell you I'm at home. Under those special circumstances, that mushroom *does* mean something. It's also conceivable – if highly unlikely – that human life is similarly being used as a sign. For example, perhaps passing aliens seeded planet Earth with life to function as a sort of cosmic road sign, to tell alien spacecraft, 'Turn left at the next solar system'. If so, then life on Earth has a meaning. However, I doubt anyone would suppose this discovery would reveal that human life was, after all, 'meaningful'. That's just not the sort of 'meaning' we're interested in when we ask, 'What's the meaning of life?'

A related question that often crops up when the meaning of life is discussed is: What's the *purpose* of life? What's it *for*? What's *your* life for? If your life *did* have some sort of purpose, would that make it meaningful?

Not necessarily. In fact, your life *does* have a purpose. All living organisms have evolved to survive and reproduce. That's what they're 'for', at least from an evolutionary perspective. But of course, being told that my purpose, as a member of the species *homo sapiens*, is to survive long enough to successfully reproduce doesn't make my life seem particularly meaningful. After all, I share that purpose with a slug.

But perhaps we've been focused on the *wrong sort of purpose*. What if some religious folk are right and we're all *made to love God*? That's our cosmic purpose. If that was the purpose for which we are made, would it make our lives meaningful?

It's not obvious that it would. Suppose a son discovers that his mother craved the love of a child and gave birth only to satisfy that desire. That discovery is unlikely to make the son feel his life is meaningful. If anything, discovering he was created only as a means to an end, to satisfy his mother's selfish desire, might lead that son to think that his life is rather less meaningful than he'd thought. Indeed, isn't creating human beings for some *purpose* generally a rather demeaning and degrading thing to do?

So, a meaningful life is not obviously delivered by having a purpose. Nor, when we enquire into the meaning of life, are we asking about what our life means as some sort of symbol or sign (like the word 'blancmange'). But then what *are* we asking when we ask about the meaning of life?

In fact, both religious and non-religious people tend for the most part to agree about which lives are meaningful. Most of us will think of people such as Einstein,

Roald Amundsen, Mary Seacole, Mozart, Ada Lovelace and Marie Curie as having led good, and indeed meaningful, lives. A meaningful life needn't be a happy life. Nor need it lead to the success of its central project. Scott of the Antarctic famously failed to reach the South Pole – yet he is celebrated for his attempt. Nor need a meaningful life be particularly moral. I'd count one or two philandering drug addicts as having led meaningful lives, just so long as their life's project – creating music, say – wasn't a downright *im*moral one. Someone who has devoted their life to mass murder, on the other hand, surely hasn't led a meaningful life, no matter how ingeniously and successfully they carried out their awful plan.

So, it seems we can recognise meaningful lives when we see them. But then it seems that, in a sense, we already know what marks them out as meaningful. The difficulty comes in pinning down precisely what's required for a meaningful life. What's the *recipe*?

In asking for *the* meaning of life, aren't we asking for that *one feature* that all and only meaningful lives necessarily share – that one feature that makes them meaningful? But why must there be one feature that all and only meaningful lives share?

One of the Austrian philosopher Ludwig Wittgenstein's (1889–1951) most famous insights is that some concepts are what he calls *family resemblance concepts*. If you take a look at the faces of different members of a family, you may notice they all resemble each other. Some have the big nose, others the blue eyes, and others the wavy hair. But, despite all those overlapping similarities between the family members, there needn't be *one* facial feature – for example, that big nose – that they all have in common. Wittgenstein thought that some concepts – such as the concept of a game – are family resemblance concepts. What is it, asks Wittgenstein, that all games have in common? Some are competitive, some not. Some involve balls, others not. Some are team games, some not. Wittgenstein suggests that, again, there is no single feature all games have in common. When we look at badminton, backgammon, football, solitaire, and chess, we find, not *one feature common to all of them*, but rather a *series of overlapping similarities*. Yet, despite there being no such single common denominator, the concept of a *game* is both legitimate and useful.

So perhaps, in looking for the one feature that makes lives meaningful, we are setting off on a wild goose chase. Perhaps here, too, we will find not a single essential feature that all meaningful lives share, but rather a series of overlapping similarities.

In which case, asking for *the* meaning of life may be symptomatic of a confusion: of assuming there must be some hidden single, essential, underlying feature that makes lives meaningful, if only we could identify what it was. When we fail to locate this one feature, we may jump

15. Why have I never been asked out?

Why am I never asked out? Why don't other people desire me? Am I unattractive? What's the *matter* with me? These are some of the thoughts to which we are prone, particularly when we're young and we see others starting out on their romantic relationships. I certainly had such thoughts myself.

Personally, I would have loved to have been asked out when I was at school, but never was. That said, I didn't ask anyone out either. My problem was the usual one: *I was afraid*. No one wants to face a humiliating rejection. Consequently, people I would dearly have liked to take out on a date never got asked.

But then one of the main reasons you haven't been asked out yet has little to do with you, and much to do with others. They're frightened to ask. Still, the solution lies in your hands. Why do you assume it has to be *them* that asks *you*? Why can't you ask them? You can!

One of the cheesier bits of philosophical advice we give each other is: *carpe diem*! Seize the day! The expression was first uttered by the Ancient Roman poet Horace over 2,000 years ago, and it has since found its way into all sorts of strange places, such as onto the wrist of actress Dame Judi Dench. Dench had 'Carpe Diem' tattooed there on her eighty-first birthday. We also say: 'Yolo!' (you only live once), encouraging others to be brave and take the plunge. And of course Nike billboards say: 'Just Do It.'

Cheesy advice it may be, but sometimes 'seize the day!' is exactly what you should do. Obviously, taking the plunge when you don't fully understand the risks is generally bad advice. 'Seize the day!' has spurred young people into foolish acts of bravado by diving into opaque and unfamiliar water, for example. But other times, when the risks are clear, taking the plunge is good advice. The truth is that, though the prospect might be terrifying, there's usually little *real* risk in asking someone out. The worst that can happen is that you get rejected. And even then there may be an upside. You may develop a reputation for 'bottle'. Remember too that you'll probably make the other person's day. Even if they don't take up your invitation, they may well be flattered.

Why have I never been asked out?

The French existentialist philosophers may also have some relevant advice. Jean-Paul Sartre (1905–1980), for example, argues that we are all fundamentally free creatures able to choose how we live. However, we can find this freedom, and the responsibility for choosing what comes with it, deeply disturbing. As a consequence, we pretend to ourselves that we have no choice, that we are ordained to play a role. Sartre encourages us to see that the social roles we adopt – of mother, woman, chef, waiter, priest and so on – do not define us. Though we might like to tell ourselves, 'This is what I am – a waiter – and this is what I must do: take the orders and bring food', the truth is that we're not defined by these roles and can, at any moment, break free and live a more authentic existence. Sartre calls this sort of role-play designed to hide our freedom from ourselves 'bad faith'.

The feminist philosopher Simone de Beauvoir (1908–1986) went on to apply this idea of 'bad faith' to women, suggesting that they can act in bad faith by playing the roles traditionally assigned to them by men. So, might there not be a little philosophical 'bad faith' involved when a woman asks herself, 'Why hasn't anyone asked me out?' Isn't she assuming that, as a woman, she's someone *to whom life merely happens*, rather than someone *who makes things happen*? Isn't she assuming that this is her allotted role which she must accept? If so,

▶ Result

Bullshit is everywhere: in politics, on the internet, in marketing, in public relations. You can't avoid it. Books such as James Ball's *Post-Truth: How Bullshit Conquered the World* and Evan Davis's *Post-Truth: Why We Have Reached Peak Bullshit and What We Can Do About It* warn that we're entering a new 'post-truth' era in which bullshit reigns.

What is bullshit? According to American philosopher Harry Frankfurt, bullshitters don't care whether what they say is true or not. It's not that bullshitters are liars. Liars know the truth, and deliberately try to persuade you to believe what they know is false. Bullshitters, on the other hand, say things for effect, whether they're true or not.

Donald Trump has been accused of being both a liar and a bullshitter. Matthew d'Ancona, in his book *Post Truth: The New War on Truth*, provides one example.

Trump claims in his book *Trump: The Art of the Deal* that the decorative tiles in the children's room at Mar-a-Lago, Trump's beach club, were made personally by Walt Disney. When Trump's butler asked him if this was actually true, Trump replied 'Who cares?'

Frankfurt thinks that bullshitters are *worse* than liars. The honest person and the liar are at least both focused on what's true and false. The honest person says what they think is true; the liar says what they think is false. The bullshitter, on the other hand:

> … is neither on the side of the true nor on the side of the false. His eye is not on the facts at all, as the eyes of the honest man and of the liar are, except insofar as they may be pertinent to his interest in getting away with what he says. He does not care whether the things he says describe reality correctly. He just picks them out, or makes them up, to suit his purpose.[26]

Why do bullshitters bullshit? Usually, for personal gain. Sometimes there's money to be made. Bullshitters may charge for their bullshit mechanical, medical, or plumbing advice, or charge extra for the antique they just made the centrepiece of some bullshit story. Bullshit is often also about *status*. Bullshitters often feign knowledge to enhance their status as 'expert'. Take, for example, the pseudo-intellectual dinner party guest who proclaims, 'As Descartes said ...', while being unsure whether Descartes said it or not. Trump's bullshit about the decorative tiles at his Mar-a-Lago resort ticks both these boxes: it was self-aggrandising and also increased the value of his Florida property.

Why should we care about bullshit? One obvious reason is: if you listen to bullshitters, you're likely to end up believing many falsehoods, and those falsehoods may hurt you. Bullshit mechanical advice may lead you to drive a dangerously unreliable car. Bullshit medical advice may damage your health. Bullshit financial advice may bankrupt you.

Although Frankfurt identifies one important type of bullshit, I suggest other things go by the same name. According to Frankfurt, the bullshitter *doesn't care* whether what they say is true or false. But is that always true? Consider feng shui, astrology, psychic powers, astral healing, alien abductions, anti-vaxxers, weird religious cults, and belief in a flat Earth. These belief systems are often classed as bullshit. Yet it's clear that many of those who sign up to and promote them often care passionately about their truth.

Some may be tempted to say that believers in these kooky beliefs are deceiving themselves and others. Frankfurt is right: they don't *really* care about what's true and what's not. They just talk and act as if they do. But in many cases that strikes me as highly implausible. For notice that the True Believers are sometimes prepared to *bet their own lives, and even the lives of their children,* on the truth of what they claim.

Consider suicide cultists, like the followers of the self-styled Reverend Jim Jones, whose community of over 900 followers (including 304 children) committed mass suicide in 'Jonestown' in the Guyanan jungle. Jim Jones's religious cult was surely a bullshit system of belief, despite the fact that those promoting it were so convinced it was true they were prepared to die for it.

Or consider 'anti-vaxxers': people who oppose vaccinating folk, including their own children, against polio, measles, typhoid and other diseases. Anti-vaxxers are prepared to bet their children's lives on the truth of their anti-vax beliefs. Calling out as 'bullshit' these and other examples of what we consider to be flaky and/or pseudo-scientific belief systems is, it seems to me, a typical and entirely proper way of using the term, despite the fact that their followers often care deeply about whether the beliefs are true, and indeed are prepared to bet everything on their truth.

Being able to spot bullshit when you come across it is an important life skill. It might even save your life. But how do you develop a nose for it?

Spotting bullshit is partly a matter of developing a nose for what's true. It's about developing good critical thinking skills and habits, so that you don't just passively accept what you are told, but can ask one or two penetrating questions of the bullshitter, such as *'How* do you know that's true?' and 'Do you have some *evidence* for that?' It's also, in part, about getting a sense of how the world works, politically, socially, and scientifically, so that you can spot when what the bullshitter claims is a poor fit with reality.

Spotting bullshit is also about developing a nose for character. I suggest there are three kinds of character to watch out for. First, there's the *Egoist*: the Frankfurt-style bullshitter who is self-aggrandising and who will say whatever will enhance their status, be it true or false. Second, there's the *Weasel*: the other sort of Frankfurt-style bullshitter who is on the make and who will say whatever is required to part you from your cash. Third, there's the *True Believer*. The True Believer may be entirely generous and sincere, and very much concerned about saying and believing what's true. However, they're gullible: the victim of a flaky belief system that has made an intellectual prisoner of them. When you can spot the Egoist, the Weasel, and the True Believer at some distance, you'll be much more immune to bullshit.

17. Are some conspiracy theories true?

Many people believe that the condensation trails made by airliners are actual plumes of chemicals – 'chemtrails'–created by secret government programmes. Surprisingly large numbers believe the Moon landings were faked by NASA and the US government. Many believe the destruction of the Twin Towers on 9/11 was an 'inside job' by the US government and involved a controlled demolition. Other popular conspiracy theories are that 2012 massacre at Sandy Hook Elementary School in Connecticut, USA was faked to promote gun control, that the pharmaceutical industry has covered up the fact that some vaccinations cause autism, that an alien spaceship crashed at Roswell and is currently stored in a place called Area 51, and that the Kennedy assassination was a conspiracy involving multiple shooters.

Why are we drawn to conspiracy theories? Research suggests a combination of three things. First, we want to *understand how the world works*. Conspiracy theories offer us narratives that explain events in an easy-to-understand way: powerful secret plotters are orchestrating them. Second, we want to *feel secure and in control*. Conspiracy theories often offer us a fairly simple recipe for taking back control: we must overthrow those powerful secret plotters. Third, conspiracy theories *enhance our own self-image*: as a conspiracy theorist, you enter into a world of like-minded insiders who can see how things *really* are – unlike the poor, deluded saps on the outside.

To call a belief a 'conspiracy theory' is often a way of dismissing it out of hand. The 'conspiracy theorist' is widely perceived to be paranoid and unhinged. Despite their popularity, all the conspiracy theories outlined above are widely considered to be nonsense.

The term 'conspiracy theory' is used in various ways. Some use 'conspiracy theory' so that, by definition, a conspiracy theory is either false or at least not well supported by evidence. In the unlikely event that any of the above theories was shown to be true, it would then cease to qualify as a 'conspiracy theory'. Some use 'conspiracy theory' in an even more restricted way, so that only theories that are completely cranky qualify.

However, others, myself included, say that what makes a theory a 'conspiracy theory' is just its content, irrespective of how reasonable or unreasonable it might happen to be. By a 'conspiracy theory', I mean a theory that posits a major conspiracy – a secret plot by some influential body and group to do something illegal, harmful or at least frowned upon – *whether or not the theory is true or well supported*. So, on my use of the term, a conspiracy theory *can* be both reasonable and true (even if most aren't).

Actually, every now and then a conspiracy theory *is* revealed to be true. For example, Watergate was a secret conspiracy within the US Republican Party – including President Nixon – to bug Democrat offices and later cover it up. This exciting story became the focus of a film called *All The President's Men*, but the theory was true. Iran–Contra was a secret conspiracy by senior officials under Reagan to sell arms to Iran, despite that being illegal, and then to use the profits to fund the right-wing Contra rebel groups in Nicaragua. Again, this conspiracy theory was true.

Still, many conspiracy theories are false and poorly supported. In fact, just a little common sense can often reveal that a conspiracy theory is unlikely to be true.

Take for example the theory that 9/11 was an inside job. The main evidence for this theory is that various features of the event are supposedly otherwise difficult to explain, such as the way the Twin Towers came down after the planes hit them. They came straight down, just like in a controlled demolition. But now consider how elaborate and huge the conspiracy would have to be. Many thousands of people would need to be in on it, including the teams that placed the explosives undetected inside the towers, the pilots who killed themselves (why would they do that?), or, if the aircraft were remote controlled, the various teams required on the ground, including at airports. The chances of such an elaborate plot failing or being exposed by a slip up or someone spilling the beans would be huge. If the aim of 9/11 was to legitimise going to war in Iraq and Afghanistan, say, then why have the planes being flown by Saudis? But, perhaps most problematic of all, *why choose such an extraordinarily risky and elaborate method of justifying going to war when far, far simpler and less risky ways of achieving that same result were available?* While it's *possible* 9/11 was an inside job – and while it's *possible* there are fairies at the bottom of the garden – the evidence in each case points strongly against it.

However, while 9/11 is highly unlikely to have been an inside job, so-called 'false flag' operations aren't entirely mythical. A 'false flag' operation involves mounting an attack on yourself or your allies while disguised as the enemy. 9/11 conspiracy theorists typically believe 9/11 was a false flag operation: a US attack on the US disguised to look like an attack by foreigners.

Interestingly, the US military have planned such false flag attacks in the past. In the 1960s, the US Joint Chiefs of Staff signed off a plot to commit hijackings and bombings and plant misleading evidence that the attacks were mounted by Castro's Cuba. Operation Northwoods, as it was known, was designed to justify a US invasion of Cuba to change the regime. The attacks never took place, but, under a different president, they might have done.

World War II began with a false flag operation. In 1939, before the German invasion of Poland, Nazi soldiers and intelligence officers dressed in Polish military uniforms carried out attacks against German targets, leaving behind dead 'Polish' soldiers who were actually concentration camp victims. These attacks were then used by Hitler to justify his invasion.

So, conspiracy theories *can* turn out to be true. One or two *have* turned out to be true. Of course it's important we control our tendency to see conspiracies everywhere – a tendency that in some folk has clearly run completely out of control. But let's not forget that, occasionally, conspiracies happen.

18. Why are people religious?

▶ Result

<u>Why do people hold religious beliefs?</u> Ask a religious person why they believe and they'll probably say, 'For the same reason I believe the Earth is round and water is wet – *because my religious beliefs are both reasonable and true!*' Fair enough: if one religion is true, and someone has good grounds for believing it's true, then that would neatly explain why they believe it.

But what if I believe mine is the one true religion? How do I then explain why people believe in all the *other* religions? It can't be because they're all true too. It seems I'll need some other explanation.

Those sceptical about religious belief often insist *wishful thinking* is at the bottom of all religious belief. It's true that people often desperately want their religion to be true. That religious belief helps us cope with our fears – particularly our fear of death – is one of the most popular explanations for belief. Here, for example, is British philosopher Bertrand Russell (1872–1970) on religion:

> Religion is based, I think, primarily and mainly upon fear. It is partly the terror of the unknown, and partly, as I have said, the wish to feel that you have a kind of elder brother who will stand by you in all your troubles and disputes. Fear is the basis of the whole thing – fear of the mysterious, fear of defeat, fear of death.[27]

Others sceptical about religious belief offer further explanations. Richard Dawkins, a scientist and one of the world's best-known atheists, suggests that religions are, in effect, *viruses of the mind*.[28]

Consider a computer virus. Once the virus has got itself installed on a computer it starts to replicate, sending copies of itself out to infect new computers. Dawkins suggests religious belief spreads in a similar fashion. Religions spread, not because – like, scientifically credible beliefs – they're reasonable, well-tested, and so on, but rather because they embody the coded instruction 'spread me'. Someone infected with the 'virus' of religious belief will typically work to infect others with the same belief.

Dawkins points out other similarities between computer viruses and religious beliefs. He notes that, just as computer viruses often work to disable anti-viral software, so religious beliefs tend to be effective at disabling whatever might neutralise them, such as scientific thinking and critical scrutiny. For example, Dawkins suggests religions often make a virtue of 'faith', by which he means believing *despite a lack of*, or perhaps even *in the teeth of*, the available evidence.

A computer virus is a bad thing. In comparing religions to computer viruses, Dawkins is obviously suggesting that religions are a bad thing too. But what of the *benefits* religions bring – both to individuals and to communities? Might these benefits not explain why people believe in them?

According to some research, whether or not religious belief is true, it does at least tend to make us happier and healthier.[29] Religion can also function as a powerful social adhesive. Communities that share a religion tend to be more tightly knit. There's also evidence that the actively religious tend to have more children. But then, given that sharing a religious belief with our community might actually benefit us, at least in terms of improving our chances of surviving and reproducing, might we not have *evolved* to be religious?

Yet another intriguing explanation for religious belief is that religions are a by-product of certain cognitive mechanisms that we've evolved for other reasons. One of the most intriguing of these explanations suggests we have an HADD or *Hyperactive Agency Detection Device*. According to some evolutionary psychologists, humans have evolved to be overly sensitive to other *agents* – beings with beliefs and desires on which they act. It's certainly hugely to our advantage to be aware of the presence of other agents. They might be friends who can help us, or foes who might harm us. They might even be predators, such as tigers, who will eat us.

So, *under*-detecting other agents is quite likely to be costly. On the other hand, *over*-detecting other agents – believing they are present when they're not – is much less likely to be costly. Consequently, we've evolved to err heavily on the side of over-detection. We're highly prone to false positive beliefs in the presence of other agents. And this, according to some, at least partly explains why we humans are so prone to false beliefs in *invisible* agents, such as ghosts, dead ancestors, spirits, angels, demons, and even gods.

Suppose, for example, that you hear a rustle in the bushes when you're walking home alone in the dark. Your first involuntary thought is likely to be: 'There's someone there!' That's your HADD switching on. If you investigate the bushes and can't spot anyone, you might still suspect there's an agent present, only they're currently *not visible*. So a belief in non-visible agents is a natural by-product of our possessing an HADD. And a belief in gods is, of course, just another example of belief in invisible agency.[30]

Supposing that one of these various scientific explanations for religious belief actually turned out to be true; what would it show so far as the truth of religious belief is concerned? Would science have effectively not just explained, but *explained away*, religious belief? Would we have finally revealed that religion is nonsense?

Actually, the mere fact that science has explained why we believe something isn't *generally* thought to show that the belief isn't true. Perhaps science can explain why I believe I can hear an orchestra playing by pointing to the sound waves travelling through the air, the effect those waves are having on my ear drums, the resulting neural stimulation, and so on. The correctness of this explanation wouldn't show that I'm *not* listening to an orchestra, or that I am *deluded* about there being an orchestra there. So why should the correct scientific explanation of religious belief reveal that religious belief is delusional?

Just how much of a threat such scientific explanations are to religious belief remains a matter of debate.

Q 19. Why don't people like me?

You think people don't like you? Well, they may not *dislike* you. They may just not notice you. In a school classroom, a few will tend to stand out because of their self-confidence. Those who are shy may not be actively *dis*liked, but they may well feel lonely and ignored, as if they're nonentities.

Still, as we go through life, some people inevitably will take against us. That won't necessarily be our fault. People may take a dislike to us because of our beliefs, out of jealousy and resentment, or because we're an obstacle to something they want. We all have to put up with the fact that not everyone is going to like us, and that at least some are going to positively dislike us.

But what if *most* people dislike like you? Actually, you're in pretty good company.

105

The Ancient Greek philosopher Socrates (c. 470–399 BC) was hugely disliked by his fellow citizens, to the point that they eventually executed him. Socrates left no writings of his own, but he was a real philosopher who features in Plato's dialogues as a character. The dialogues reveal that Socrates was interested in questions such as: What is courage? What is justice? What is beauty? What is knowledge? He would engage others in conversation, often asking the supposed experts his questions.

For example, Socrates asks the Athenian general Laches what courage is. Socrates then discovers that he can always come up with *counterexamples* to the answers Laches provides. Laches, for instance, starts off by defining courage as holding your position in combat. Socrates points out he wants a definition that applies not just to soldiers but to all situations in life. Even civilians can be courageous. So Laches then suggests that courage is 'a certain perseverance of the soul': the courageous just *keep going*. Socrates shoots this second definition down too, pointing out that sometimes the prudent thing to do is *not* to persevere come what may, but to retreat and live to fight another day. If courage is a virtue, it can't be foolhardy, and it's foolhardy to pointlessly fight to the death. So it appears Socrates has shown that Laches is again mistaken: there's more to courage than just a certain sort of perseverance.

Why don't people like me?

It's embarrassing to be shown that you can't even define the thing you're supposed to be an expert on. Laches no doubt felt irritated by Socrates' probing questions and ripostes. Socrates similarly embarrassed and humiliated many influential people. In fact, he famously likened himself to a gadfly pricking and stinging a horse. The horse will soon want to swat and kill that fly. Eventually, the great and good of Athens wanted Socrates swatted too.

Socrates didn't *intend* to make people dislike him. He just wanted to find out what courage, beauty and knowledge *really* are, and ended up concluding that neither he nor the supposed experts knew. Still, as a result of his relentlessly pursuing this noble project, he made powerful enemies. Socrates was eventually put on trial for crimes including 'corrupting the youth'. He was found guilty and condemned to death. Though he was given a chance to escape, Socrates chose to stay in his prison cell, drink the hemlock offered him, and die. Plato's dialogue *The Apology* tells the story of Socrates' final hours in his cell in the company of close friends.

So, even a noble soul like Socrates can find that most people actively dislike him, precisely because he *is* a noble soul engaged on a worthwhile project. And of course Socrates isn't alone. Taking a principled stand and fighting for what's right often makes people highly unpopular. Sometimes dangerously – and occasionally even fatally – unpopular. Being disliked can be a badge of honour.

Still, other people are disliked with good reason. Indeed, one or two of us really are unlikeable. If you're concerned about being unpopular, and suspect you may have flaws that explain your lack of popularity, you might find it helpful to consider the following, I think sensible, advice.

Being *self-centred* can be very off-putting to others. If you're only interested in talking about yourself – if conversations with others tend to revolve around *your* interests, *your* achievements, the great things *you* have been doing – then, especially if your monologues drift towards bragging, your audience is likely to find you an irritating bore. People liked by those they interact with are usually people genuinely interested in others. They tend to ask questions of others – about what they have been up to and how they are doing. One very obvious way of making others feel happier about being in your company is to be interested in them.

Being overly *critical of others* is also an unappealing trait. By all means be straight talking, but sniping at others is obviously eventually going to make them feel unhappy about being in your company. Are you someone who makes others feel bad about themselves? If so, you may want to change your habits. Get yourself into the routine of saying something genuine and positive about people you meet: about their appearance, their achievements and so on.

Complaining can also make people feel bad. It's good to have friends with whom we can discuss our problems, but if that's *all* we discuss with them – if we spend most of our time whingeing – then, again, we can be difficult to be around.

Some of the most irritating people are those who constantly cut us off mid-sentence. Don't *interrupt* when others are talking: listen. And I mean *really* listen. Don't just put on your 'listening' face and then start talking about your own thoughts again, but actually take on board what they are saying and engage properly with it. When they've finished speaking, don't immediately start off on your own entirely tangential monologue.

Being *boastful* is also unlikely to win you any popularity contests. Talking constantly about your new shoes, fabulous career, expensive new car, glamorous home, amazing holiday, super-achieving children at their expensive school, is only going to make others feel inadequate and second-rate. No one wants to hang around people who make them feel like that.

Avoid trying to *control other people*. By all means offer advice if it's helpful. Feel free to inspire them and point out opportunities they might not have spotted. But don't cross the line into ordering them about. No one likes to feel like they are losing their autonomy and becoming someone else's 'project'. People like being around other people who inspire and empower them; they tend to avoid those who make them feel like puppets.

Notice that many of these unpopular traits are related. Being boastful is obviously a way of being self-centred, as is endlessly complaining about your own problems. At the heart of all this advice is the thought that *being liked is in large part about liking and being interested in other people*. And notice that what makes you more popular will in many cases also make other people happier. So following the advice may well be good, not just for you, but for them too.

20. Is honesty always the best policy?

▷ Result

You've just been given a birthday gift by your
Aunt Daisy. Ripping off the paper, you discover a hideous
sweater. Aunt Daisy looks at you expectantly. 'Do you like
it?' she asks.

What do you say?

Many would lie. We'd say, 'Oh, how lovely! Just what I
needed' and reassure Aunt Daisy it was a great present.
But is that the right thing to do? Is honesty always the
best policy?

The German philosopher Immanuel Kant thought so.
According to Kant, morality takes the form of strict and
exceptionless moral rules, such as 'do not steal' and 'do
not lie'. You must never lie, no matter what the
circumstances. Suppose a mad axeman enters your
home asking where your family are hiding. Even if lying
is the only way to save them, you must not lie, says Kant.

This, most of us will conclude, is a ludicrously extreme view.

So, Kant's advice regarding that hideous sweater is, obviously: don't lie! Of course, that doesn't entail you should tell the truth. Perhaps, rather than fibbing, you could distract Aunt Daisy with a cup of tea, or say, 'Was that the phone?' and head out the door. Still, Daisy would probably guess the truth. It's likely that the only way to avoid disappointing her is to tell her a bare-faced lie. Daisy's disappointment, and indeed the death of your family at the hands of the mad axeman, may be an unfortunate *consequence* of not lying, says Kant, but *it's your duty not to lie*. The consequences of our actions, Kant insists, are always completely morally irrelevant.

The trouble is, almost no one thinks the consequences of our actions are completely morally irrelevant. Kant's view is rejected by most of us, and certainly by 'consequentialist' philosophers like the English thinker John Stuart Mill (1806–1873), who says that, actually, *all* that matters, morally speaking, is the consequences of our actions. But what consequences? For Mill, the answer is: the *consequences regarding happiness*. The right thing to do, morally speaking, is to do whatever will produce the happiest outcome.

What does this particular consequentialist view, called *utilitarianism*, require you to do about Aunt Daisy's gift? Should you lie, or not? According to the utilitarian, you must perform a calculation. You must consider the consequences of lying and not lying, and do what you calculate will produce the happiest outcome. If you predict that Aunt Daisy will be distraught if you tell the truth about the sweater, whereas she, and everyone else, will be happier if you lie, then you should lie. Or so says this simple form of utilitarianism.

One difficulty we now face, however, is that calculating which action will produce the happiest outcome is tricky. If you lie to Aunt Daisy, she may be happy now, but then, later, she may discover the truth and be even more upset. Or perhaps she already suspects she's buying gifts you don't like, and this is causing her anguish which could be avoided if you just told the truth. And if you're honest with Aunt Daisy, *you* might be happier too: you can now receive gifts you actually like, and won't have to feel bad about lying. Balancing all these factors up is no easy task.

Utilitarianism has its critics. Is it best to deceive if that's what makes people happiest overall? The American philosopher Robert Nozick (1938–2002) imagines a hypothetical device called the 'experience machine', which can produce any experience you like at the press of a button (we considered a version of this machine earlier, in 'Why don't I enjoy life?', page 43). Think of this machine as creating virtual *Matrix*-like worlds in which you can immerse yourself. You can experience whatever sensory or other delights you want. You can eat the most delicious foods, engage in erotic romps with whomever you please, or listen to opera – whatever takes your fancy. But now suppose you have the option of locking unsuspecting people into this machine for the rest of their lives. They are going to be deliriously happy, let's suppose. Particularly if they think that what they're experiencing is real, which – let's also suppose – they will.

So, *if you imprison people inside the machine, you increase happiness overall.* But is that morally the right thing to do? Surely not. Yes, people are happier, but life is not all about being happy, is it? We also want to have experiences that are authentic. In particular, we want to have real achievements, not fake ones. Someone who has lived out their life blissfully unaware that all their relationships were fake, their partner didn't really exist, and that their proudest achievements – climbing Mount Everest, and raising two beautiful children – were all a lie, has surely missed out on something hugely important, whether they realise it or not. Living an authentic existence is something most of us value even more highly than happiness – certainly if happiness is understood as 'feeling good'. The German philosopher Friedrich Nietzsche (1844–1900) once said, 'Mankind does not strive for happiness; only the Englishman does', clearly referring to utilitarians like Mill.

Of course, none of this is to say that feeling good doesn't matter *at all*, morally speaking. Yes, Kant was probably wrong to say that the consequences of our actions are *completely* irrelevant so far as what we morally ought to do is concerned. Surely we do need to consider the effects our actions will have on the happiness and well being of others. But it seems to me, and many others, that happiness isn't the *only* thing we should consider when judging what is morally the right thing to do. In which case, perhaps you're going to have to tell Aunt Daisy the truth after all?

Result

<u>Suppose I'm looking at a remarkable sunset.</u> The last rays of the sun are lighting up the clouds in the most extraordinary way, and the landscape has taken on the form of a delightful silhouette. I'm blown away by the beauty of it all.

But now consider the question: *where* is the beauty? The answer, I might think, is obvious: it's in the sunset! It's *that sunset* that's beautiful. But others contradict me: 'No. The beauty isn't in the sunset, it's in *the eye of the beholder*. It's in you!'

What on Earth do they mean by this? The thought seems to be that while some properties really are 'out there' – independently of us and our minds – others aren't. The sunset has various properties, such as appearing at a certain time, exhibiting certain shapes, and so on. These properties really are 'out there' independently of the mind of any observer. However, the property of being beautiful isn't 'out there'. It's 'in us'.

A similar view is often expressed about sounds. Does a tree that falls in the forest, when no one is around to hear it, make a sound? Some think of sound as mind-independently 'out there', while others insist that the sound is really in the ear – or perhaps the nervous system – of the hearer. If no one's there to hear the sound, there's no sound!

The Italian scientist Galileo (1564–1642) took just this view about colour. He thought that while objects have properties such as shape, size, mass, and position, they don't have colours. Colours, said Galileo, reside wholly in us, the 'observing animal so that if the animal were removed, every such quality would be abolished and annihilated'.[31]

But why should we believe that? Well, one popular reason is that science ultimately explains everything in terms of measurable properties such as shape, size, mass, and position. Scientific explanation, it's claimed, makes no appeal to colour. This, it's suggested, is good reason to suppose that colour isn't fully and objectively 'out there' in the way those other properties are.

There's certainly no reason to assume that our various senses must represent the world as it really is in every respect. To some extent, appearances are misleading. So perhaps our senses gild and stain a world that, stripped bare of the contribution made by our own minds, is much more austere. Perhaps we mistakenly 'project' onto the world a great deal of what, in truth, lies in us.

The view that colours, sounds, beauty, and other properties such as smells, tastes, deliciousness, and disgustingness, are essentially mind-dependent is called *anti-realism*. On the subject of beauty, anti-realists would say that the beauty of that sunset is actually dependent on the mind of observers such as myself.

However, do we really want to say that, in the absence of observers, things aren't actually coloured, smelly, or noisy? In fact, there is an interesting philosophical halfway position on colours and sounds that, while still anti-realist, allows for at least a *degree* of mind-independence.

Take, for example, the philosopher John Locke's theory of colour. According to one of Locke's two definitions of colour, colour consists in a *power or disposition* of an object to produce a certain sensation or appearance in us. Now, dispositions can be present even when they're not doing anything.

Take a sugar cube. It has the dispositional property of being soluble. Its being soluble consists in the fact that it will dissolve if placed in water. The sugar cube has that disposition right now, even though it's not actually dissolving now. In fact, it has the property even if it *never* dissolves because it gets smashed by a hammer instead.

Similarly if colours are just *dispositions that objects have to produce certain sensations or appearances in us*, then they can be coloured *even when we're not looking at them*. In fact, they can be coloured even if *no one ever looks at them*. This fits with common sense: a poppy can be red even when we're not looking at it. It can be red even if no one *ever* looks at it.

Still, Locke's dispositional theory of colour is anti-realist. It still makes colour mind-dependent. To see why, imagine that alien creatures look at a poppy. For us humans, the poppy is red – because it produces a certain sensory appearance in us (call that appearance 'R'). But suppose that, because they have different nervous systems, the poppy produces a different sensory appearance in the aliens. It produces not R, but the appearance we get when we look at grass (call this appearance 'G'). Then Locke's view has the consequence that while, for us, poppies are red, for the aliens, they're green. We're both correct! There's no fact of the matter as to what colour poppies are *really*, independently of any observer. The colour of a poppy is *relative to the audience*. So, colour *is* still mind-dependent, according to Locke's view.

So, even if you think poppies are red when no one looks at them – even if you think a poppy can be red even if no one ever looks at it – you can still be an anti-realist about colour. The same is true of sound. You can suppose that a tree falling in a forest does make a sound even if there's no one there to hear it, and yet still think of sound as mind-dependent, if you suppose sound is just a *disposition* to produce a certain auditory experience. We could take this view about beauty too: the sunset is beautiful and would be beautiful even if there was no one to see it. But still, its beauty is tied essentially to the subjective. And what's beautiful for us might be ugly for aliens.

If you're tempted by anti-realist thoughts about beauty, colour, and sounds, then what about morality? Is the wrongness of an act of murder or theft in the action itself, or in the eye of the onlooker? The philosopher David Hume famously took an anti-realist view about morality. He said that when you try to find the 'vice' or wrongness of an act by looking at the act, you can never find it, 'till you turn your reflexion into your own breast and find a sentiment of disapprobation, which arises in you, towards this action … It lies in yourself, not in the object.'[32]

Or, if you're willing to consider a *really* bold version of anti-realism, consider the Irish philosopher George Berkeley (1685–1753), who convinced himself that not only are colours, tastes, and sounds not 'out there' mind-independently, *nor are physical objects*. Physical objects, thought Berkeley, exist only in the mind of observers. If you ask Berkeley, 'If a tree falls in a forest and no one hears it, does it make a sound?' Berkeley will insist that if no one observes the tree falling, then not only is there no sound, *there is no tree*. Nothing exists but minds and their perceptions. The only reason Berkeley allows that trees can continue to exist when we're not looking at them is that he supposes that God continues to look at them. God's unwavering gaze keeps the entire *universe* in existence!

Just how realist, or anti-realist, are you? Do you think trees that fall unheard make a sound? Do you believe unseen things coloured? Do you suppose the entire contents of your fridge disappear when you shut the door? Do you suppose beauty is in the eye of the beholder?

22. Why is the world such a mess?

In asking 'Why is the world such a mess?' we may mean: why isn't it *better than it actually is*? There's the way the world *should* be, and then there's how it actually is, which falls far short of that ideal. So the question is, *why* does it fall short? This is often how religious people frame the question, of course.

On the other hand, if someone tips out a drawer on to the floor and surveys the resulting chaos, they're unlikely to be struck by the question 'Why is all this stuff in such a mess?' *Of course* it's a mess. What else would you expect if you tip out the contents of a drawer? The chaos you survey is precisely what you should expect. In fact, what would be really weird is if the contents of the tipped-out drawer *weren't* a mess. If all the clothes landed neatly folded into piles, and the other contents fell sorted neatly into colour co-ordinated rows, now that really would need explaining. But if they fell into a mess? Nothing mysterious about that.

Similarly, if we think of humanity as the result of natural selection, random forces, and chance, why should we be surprised that humanity ends up in something of a mess? Isn't that what we should expect?

On the other hand, if you think of the world as the product of some sort of plan – perhaps God's plan – a plan that specifies how things *should* be, then you're likely to think: *this isn't how things are supposed to be*. So you might well ask: 'Why isn't the world the way it's supposed to be?'

The answer is: because *we're flawed human beings*. We are prone to selfish, short-term thinking, to anger and even violence when we don't get our way. Yes, maybe the world *should* be better. Maybe we, or God, *planned* and *intended* for it to be better, but, being all-too-human, we've screwed up. That we're flawed human beings is something on which religious people and atheists usually agree, even if they disagree on why we're flawed. Some believe we're flawed because we've inherited the original sin of Adam and Eve; others believe we're flawed because we've evolved that way.

Another way of asking the question 'Why is the world such a mess?' is to contrast it with how it *once was*. Why is the world such a mess compared to the Good Ol' Days?

A few years ago I was invited to attend a conference about our 'Post Christian' future. The participants were varied, but included a large proportion of religious believers, including a number of bishops. The two-day event began, predictably, with much hand-wringing about how bad things were getting. Concerns were raised about moral decline. Indeed that was the opening theme. The general feeling was that society is undergoing a 'moral malaise'. It has lost its moral compass. But then, after two days of discussion, the conference ended with a show of hands on whether things were getting better or worse, morally speaking. Surprisingly, that final poll revealed a dramatic turn around. A clear majority now thought that, on reflection, things were rather *better* than they were fifty or a hundred years ago. Over the course of the conference, the participants had reminded themselves just how awful our moral attitudes had been towards other races, towards women, towards gay people, and other minorities and now thought that, on balance, we had as a nation become rather *more* moral, not less.

Of course, the notion that we're 'going to hell in a handcart' is widespread. Newspapers regularly paint a depressing portrait of modern Britain. Many expend a great deal of ink on such 'problems' as immigration (particularly non-white immigration), feckless spongers on benefits taking advantage of the system, rising criminality, and on the immoral and promiscuous young.

improving, crime and homicide rates are falling, famine is reducing, war is reducing, and education is improving. Though there are local blips and regressions, the overall trend is, according to Pinker, very much one of *progress*. Pinker credits science and reason for much of that progress. There's no denying science has transformed our lives in a very short period of time. Just a couple of hundred years ago there were no effective anaesthetics, little effective medicine, no electricity or refrigeration, no cars, trains, planes, computers or the internet.

When we ask, 'Why is the world such a mess?' it's worth remembering that, while it no doubt *is* in many ways pretty messy, it's also, in many important respects, improving all the time.

Still, while Pinker is correct that we are making great progress on many important fronts, there are areas of global decline. In response to Pinker, many note that inequality is rising rapidly. And that while economic progress has been made, it has been made at the expense of an environment that is now at crisis point. It's also worth remembering that while we humans may be experiencing progress, many other species aren't so lucky. We are living through a vast, human-caused 'die-off'. The ecologist Stuart Pimm argues that species are going extinct at a rate 1,000 times higher than the natural background rates and that future rates are likely to be 10,000 times higher.

23. When will my life begin?

Many of us feel we're stalled on the hard shoulder of life, watching in frustration as others whizz past towards their chosen destinations. We just can't seem to get anywhere. This feeling can be particularly acute around New Year. Another year has passed and what progress have I made? Perhaps very little. We may try to kick-start things by making New Year resolutions, insisting that this year, we really, really, *really* are going to start getting fit, get a new qualification, find a life partner, or get that better job. Yet we often grind to a halt again.

So, what's the secret to getting things moving?

Perhaps we need to focus on developing better habits. According to the American philosopher and psychologist William James (1842–1910), the secret to forming good character does not lie in forming the right *sentiments* or *intentions*: 'With mere good intentions, hell is proverbially paved.' No matter how sincere and passionate you may be right now, merely telling yourself 'This year I am *definitely, absolutely* going to … ' is unlikely to have much effect. James thought that the key to success lies instead in developing good habits, and he illustrates the power of habit with an anecdote:

> There is a story, which is credible enough, though it may not be true, of a practical joker, who, seeing a discharged veteran carrying home his dinner, suddenly called out, 'Attention!' whereupon the man instantly brought his hands down, and lost his mutton and potatoes in the gutter. The drill had been thorough, and its effects had become embodied in the man's nervous system.[34]

When behaviour has become habituated, it requires little effort or thought. James believes we should aim to drill ourselves in behaving in ways that are advantageous to us, so that the behaviour becomes automatic:

> The great thing … in all education, is to make our nervous system our ally instead of our enemy … For this we must make automatic and habitual, as early as possible, as many useful actions as we can … The more details of our daily life we can hand over to the effortless custody of automatism,

the more our higher powers of mind will be set free for their proper work.[35]

The idea that the development of good habits is the key to success is commonplace and a theme of many self-improvement philosophies and books. I've no doubt there's some truth to them.

Often, it's not just that we lack good habits; we've also acquired bad habits that are holding us back. We can easily fall into routines that trap us, like a hamster in its exercise wheel. We expend a great deal of energy but never actually get anywhere. Reprogramming those bad habits can take considerable effort. It's much easier to raise a young person with good habits than to have to correct the bad ones they've already acquired.

Assuming you've got into some habits that are holding you back and that you want to change, it can be helpful to make a schedule and stick to it. For example, if you want to get fit, don't just join a gym and promise yourself you'll go two or three times a week; *schedule* gym visits at specific times on specific days. Put them into your electronic diary with alerts, and then stick religiously to that pattern. It won't be long before you find yourself getting ready with little effort, for that has become your routine. You can usefully schedule other things too like social activities and study times. In this way we can, as James says, 'make our nervous system our ally instead of our enemy'.

The fact that you have acquired habits that have caught you in a rut isn't the only reason you might feel you're unable to make progress. Other reasons include nervousness about committing to a plan of action. Some of us won't make a move until everything is fully planned out and we are entirely confident both that we have the right plan and that it will succeed. However, it's rare that we can be completely sure about how things will turn out. Plans often go awry. Our situation often changes in ways we can't predict. There's always an element of doubt about whether we've chosen the right path. Risk is unavoidable. And so, if we're overly cautious, we can effectively hobble ourselves.

Fear of failure can be a particularly big obstacle to achieving anything (see 'What if I fail?', page 177). We all fail a lot. Give up after a few failures and you're bound never to get anywhere: to be left behind on the hard shoulder of life while others whizz past. Persistence is essential.

We all get angry. We lose our keys. Our computer crashes at the worst possible moment. Someone steals our parking space. Suddenly, we feel that rising tide of rage. It is an entirely natural reaction. But what if that feeling never went away? Some of us appear to live our lives permanently furious. If you feel angry all or most of the time, what should you do about it?

Of course, someone's being angry for much of the time is often easily explained. If someone has suffered a grave, ongoing injustice – perhaps they've been falsely imprisoned – then they're obviously likely to feel deeply angry. A person who has experienced something horrendous in their past may also be left with feelings of anger that won't subside. Anger can also be caused by an internal hormonal or other imbalance. If you feel angry for much of the time, it could be for one of these three reasons. If so, then you may be able to get some effective help, perhaps from a lawyer, therapist, or doctor.

What about philosophy? Has philosophy anything to offer the enraged? The Stoics thought so. One of the great Roman Stoic philosophers, Seneca the Younger (c. 4 BC–AD 65), thought that anger was a kind of temporary madness. He said that though 'other vices affect our judgement, anger affects our sanity'.[36] Seneca thought that we should *never* act on the basis of rage.

A key Stoic thought is that we need to apply reason to figure out how the world actually works, rather than how we wish it would work, so that that we don't become frustrated, angry, and suffer other negative consequences when things don't go the way we want. The Greek Stoic philosopher Epictetus (c. AD 55–135) put it well: 'We must make the best of those things that are in our power, and take the rest as nature gives it.'[37] The true Stoic is one who shows fortitude and self-control, who masters their own destructive emotions, and who uses reason as best they can in approaching life's problems.

Suppose, for example, that your car breaks down on the way to an important job interview. You've called for roadside assistance and done everything else you can to try to ensure that you make it to the interview on time. At this point, you're in the hands of fate. Many of us would feel both anxious and angry in this situation, but these negative emotions won't help at all. In fact they'll probably make your situation worse. The Stoic, at this point, aims to be calm, collected, and accepting of what they can't now change. When we find we can do nothing to alter our bad situation, we must change *ourselves*, so that it no longer causes us suffering.

Here's another example: if you go on Twitter, you're quite likely to encounter others behaving badly, in some cases going out of their way to insult or troll you. They're filled with Hulk-like rage and it's easy to find yourself becoming enraged too. In fact, that's often what the trolls want. The Stoic's advice is: don't allow such insults to affect you. Epictetus goes further and suggests that the hurt caused by insults is actually caused by *ourselves*. For we *allow* the insult to hurt us. If instead we are rock-like, remaining calm and unaffected, then no matter how barbed and cruel the online trolling, it will always be harmless.

Still, isn't anger at least *sometimes* useful? If a soldier in battle is angry, might that not help him fight more effectively? If you're in a fight for your life, won't anger aid you? Seneca thought not, asking:

> Moreover, of what use is anger, when the same end can be arrived at by reason? Do you suppose that a hunter is angry with the beasts he kills? Yet he meets them when they attack him, and follows them when they flee from him, all of which is managed by reason without anger.[38]

If you're fighting for your life against an attacking wolf, you are unlikely to be at a disadvantage because you're not angry with the wolf. In fact, not only does the addition of anger to life's battle bring nothing positive, it may lead you to act impulsively and irrationally, and so blunder. It's well established among professional fighters that anger spoils good technique and puts the angry person at a disadvantage.

So, according to Seneca, anger is *never* helpful, and should always be stopped in its tracks the moment you feel it start to bubble up:

> The best plan is to reject straightway the first incentives to anger, to resist its very beginnings, and to take care not to be betrayed into it: for if once it begins to carry us away, it is hard to get back again into a healthy condition …[39]

And don't fall for the thought that it's manly to be angry, adds the Stoic Roman Emperor Marcus Aurelius (AD 121–180):

> Let this truth be present to you in the excitement of anger: that to be moved by passion is not manly. Rather, mildness and gentleness, as they are more agreeable to human nature, are also more manly. He who possesses these qualities

possesses strength, nerves, and courage, and not the man who is subject to fits of passion and discontent.[40]

Still, is it really true that anger is *never* to our benefit? Why would we humans have evolved to feel anger if it doesn't help us survive and/or reproduce?

Like other creatures, we humans have evolved to feel the emotion of anger because it triggers certain behaviours – such as snarling and lashing out – that can be to our advantage. Clearly, it's sometimes rational to act aggressively and even violently: in self-defence, for example. But we can show aggression without anger. Note that Seneca doesn't say *don't act aggressively*; he just says: *don't act out of anger*. Be like the martial artist Bruce Lee: outwardly ferocious when required, but always tranquil within.

If you do feel yourself feeling angry all the time, try what the Stoics suggest. For example, they recommend meditating on the inevitable frustrations we run into so that, when these do occur, we're prepared and won't easily succumb to anger. American philosopher Martha C. Nussbaum writes about Nelson Mandela – unjustly imprisoned by the South African regime for decades – that:

> He often said that he knew anger well, and that he had to struggle against the demand for payback in

his own personality. He reported that during his 27 years of imprisonment he had to practise a disciplined type of meditation to keep his personality moving forward and avoiding the anger trap. It now seems clear that the prisoners on Robben Island had smuggled in a copy of *Meditations* by the Stoic philosopher Marcus Aurelius, to give them a model of patient effort against the corrosions of anger.[41]

If you find yourself feeling angry much of the time, you may find that, like Mandela, you would benefit from reading the Stoics.

Stoicism is *not* about letting people walk all over you. Stoics don't say: Don't bother try to change things and just let people treat you however they want. Rather, they say: Don't waste your time fretting about what can't be changed, and when you *do* act, act not out of anger but out of reason. Stoics can be people of principle who are prepared to fight in the cause of justice and stand up against oppression.

25. Who am I?

Usually, when someone asks us who we are, we have no problem answering. We may give our name, say where we live, and perhaps talk about our job, family, and interests. Of course, if you've had a bump on the head and lost your memory, then you won't be able to provide this information. But most of us can, without any difficulty, say exactly who we are.

And yet, strangely, when this same question is asked in a 'philosophical' tone of voice, we then struggle to answer. When a priest, counsellor, or guru asks us who we *really* are, it seems they want another sort of answer. Suddenly, many of us find ourselves completely stumped by the question.

Why is that? Why don't we know who we *really* are? What is this mysterious and elusive 'real' you? And how might it be revealed? Perhaps by looking inside ourselves?

Many assume that the 'real' self is a hidden self, locked away inside us, and so best revealed by introspection. But is it?

The Scottish philosopher David Hume famously engaged in a search for his inner self. Hume turned his attention inwards and discovered various thoughts and feelings – a memory, an experience of colour, a painful sensation, and so on. However, Hume found that his 'self', thought of as a sort of extra *thing* that has those thoughts and feelings, never showed up. Because Hume believed all concepts are derived from experience, he drew the conclusion that he had no conception of any such inner soul or self. According to Hume, the 'self' isn't some *extra* thing *over and above* the inner bundle of thoughts and feelings we experience. Rather it *just is* that bundle. Unsurprisingly, this is called Hume's bundle theory of the self.

Nor is turning our attention inwards a particularly reliable guide to *what we're really like*. Many of the traits we value – including courage, fortitude, determination, and righteousness – are revealed in, indeed *consist in*, how we behave when times get tough. A courageous person is someone who, when placed in a frightening situation, behaves well.

Donald Trump recently declared about the Parkland school shooting: 'I really believe I'd run in there, even if I didn't have a weapon.'[42] While Trump may sincerely believe this, would he have run in, unarmed, to try to save those young people? The truth is, he has little idea until put in a situation like that. And nor do we. Our courage is revealed not by navel-gazing, but by our behaviour when we're placed in a demanding situation.

So, perhaps the secret to discovering the 'real' you involves not quiet contemplation, but placing yourself in tough situations that make demands of you. If you're never put in such a situation, you'll never know – which, to be fair to Trump, he acknowledged, saying: 'You never know until you're tested.'[43]

Those asking, 'But who am I *really*?' may also be asking, 'What I am here *for*?' 'What's my *purpose*?' If a child asks about a pair of scissors, 'What's this?' you'll answer by explaining what scissors are *for* – they're made to cut things. So maybe to answer the question 'What, or who, am I?' I need to figure out what I am here for – what's my purpose?

One way of answering this question might be to talk about careers: 'Currently I am a bank manager, but that's not who I *really* am. I'm really a musician – that's the job I was *made* for.' Still, I suspect most of us asking the question 'Who am I?' aren't looking for careers advice.

Of course, as we saw in 'Does my life have meaning?' (page 77), one answer to the question 'What am I here *for*?' is that we are each here to survive and reproduce –

to pass our genetic material on to the next generation. That's our allotted role so far as being a member of the species *homo sapiens* is concerned. But, while this undoubtedly is, in a sense, one of the things we are here for, I doubt it will help many answer the question 'Who am I?' It's just too prosaic. This just isn't the sort of answer for which we're searching.

Perhaps part of the reason we find the answer to the question 'Who am I?' so elusive, and end up concluding we don't know who we are, is that we're not seeing the wood for the trees.

True enough, we all play 'roles'. We all adopt differing personas in different situations. When I'm with my family I exhibit one sort of personality; when at work I adopt another more formal persona; when I'm with my friends I reveal yet another. Which is the 'real' me? Am I one of these characters, or perhaps some 'extra' persona still waiting in the wings?

The English philosopher Gilbert Ryle (1900–1976) offers a possibly helpful analogy: a couple of tourists are walking around Oxford. They look at the various colleges, departments, and so on. But then they say, 'This is all very interesting, but where's *the University*?' These tourists have made a mistake. They think the University is an 'extra' thing over and above the colleges, departments, and so on, whereas it *just is* those things. Someone who, in looking for the 'real onion', keeps peeling back the layers and ultimately finds nothing, has been looking at the real onion the whole time.

So, perhaps the real you is not an extra 'something' hidden behind what others can observe in the rich warp and weft of your day-to-day life; rather that warp and weft *just is* the real you. The real you is not a mysterious, shadowy figure standing in the wings, still waiting to appear. The real you is to be found right there in all of the various personas you publicly exhibit and the characteristics you publicly display.

But if that's true, perhaps others may know better than you who the 'real' you is?

26. What if I never find love?

 Result

<u>Chances are you've already found love.</u> You probably had loving parents, loving siblings, and may have loving close friends too. But of course, what those who say they're 'looking for love' are usually after is *romantic* love. They want a loving relationship that includes, to put it bluntly, a sexual dimension.

Of course, even that's not entirely what we're after. A series of short-term romantic relationships won't do. What those 'looking for love' usually want is a *life partner*: a single, life-long relationship with someone deeply committed to being with us both permanently and exclusively. Often, this is a person we hope to marry.

The desire for a life partner is often assumed to be stronger in women than men. There's certainly a healthy market for books aimed specifically at heterosexual women looking to find love, books with

145

titles like: *How to Find Love & Get Married!: No-Nonsense Dating for Women in Their 30s & 40s* and *Get the Guy: Use the Secrets of the Male Mind to Find, Attract and Keep Your Ideal Man*. However, research suggests men are actually just as keen to find love. Pew Research reports that young women and men are equally likely to want to marry and to believe that having a successful marriage is one of the most important things in their lives.

Of course, not everyone wants a life partner, but many do. Our question isn't about *how* to find such a partner, but about what if – given such a relationship is something we deeply desire – we never get it? What if Mr or Ms Right never shows up? What then?

Before we to try to answer that question, it's worth considering another. *Why* do many of us want such a relationship? *Why* is this something we often desire, sometimes desperately?

It appears it's at least partly a matter of biology. If we want to raise offspring successfully, having a long-term committed sexual partner is probably our best bet. So a strong desire to have such a partner is something which nature has likely selected. We've *evolved* to want a relationship. We're not alone in having that desire. Members of many other species are also programmed to seek out a mate for life, including swans, albatrosses, wolves, and gibbons.

Of course, the fact that we can scientifically explain why so many of us want a life partner doesn't invalidate it. Wanting to breathe, and to drink when we're thirsty, are also desires that come 'built in' and that can be explained scientifically. That doesn't invalidate them either.

If a widespread desire for a single, committed life partner is part of our evolutionary programming, what follows? It doesn't follow that we're stuck with this desire. At least some of our innate tendencies can be pretty successfully suppressed, if that's what we want. We're naturally disposed to various forms of bad behaviour that we can neverthe less manage pretty effectively. For example, we seem programmed to want to stuff ourselves with sugary, fatty foods at every available opportunity, yet many of us can and do learn to suppress that desire successfully.

Still, suppressing our deepest desires isn't always healthy, or even possible. It may well be that, for many of us, a deep yearning for a life partner is something we're just stuck with. It's not a desire that we can conveniently drop, or push to the back of our minds, even if we wanted to.

Supposing the desire for a life partner is a desire you can neither get rid of, nor fulfil – what then? Understandably, and inevitably, the desire will cause you distress. Still, before getting too downcast, it's worth reminding ourselves of something: what makes us happy and what we *think* will make us happy aren't always the same thing. It turns out we humans are not that good at judging what will make us happy or, indeed, miserable.

As we will see in 'Why don't I appreciate what I have?' on page 155, many of us assume that losing a leg in an accident would make us very unhappy. However, it turns out that people who have lost a limb are on average no less happy one year later than they were before. So, don't assume you must lead a miserable, unfulfilled existence if you never find love. In fact, that assumption might be an obstacle to your finding real happiness. An obsession with fulfilling one desire can often lead us to overlook other, perhaps even more promising, opportunities for fulfilment.

In particular, don't make the mistake of thinking 'If only I had *this* then all would be right with the world!' A long-term romantic partnership is no panacea. In particular, women in heterosexual relationships often have to work harder within such relationships than their male counterparts. They tend to do more of the domestic tasks as well as more of the emotional labour. Be careful what you wish for, because it may end up involving a great deal of domestic drudgery.

Many people are able to lead fulfilled, happy lives in the absence of any such relationship. This is particularly true of women. Women are happier being single than are men. They're better at socialising by themselves and are more likely to have close friends for support. Research also suggests women who lack a partner tend to engage in more social activities, whereas men without a partner tend to pursue fewer.

Yes, having to live with a deep, frustrated desire can be distressing. But remember that the fulfilment of such desires can lead to unforeseen and undesirable consequences. And above all, remember it's possible to lead a fulfilled and happy life even when a dream has been dashed. Indeed, sometimes it's only when one dream is dashed that we're able to find something equally, perhaps even more, valuable.

▶ Result

From a scientific, naturalistic perspective, the fact that the good suffer is no surprise. Indeed, that the good suffer is surely to be expected. Natural events often have dire consequences for humans and other sentient creatures. They cause diseases and bring about natural disasters, for example. Nature doesn't care about these consequences. It just relentlessly grinds them out, harming and slaughtering the good and the bad with indifference. And so, inevitably, the good suffer.

But then why do we wring our hands and ask *why* the good suffer if the answer is so blindingly obvious? The answer, I suspect, is that we're naturally drawn to the idea of some sort of *cosmic justice*. Most of us, when we see a wonderful person cursed with an awful disease, will be tempted to think: 'This is so *unfair*. Why *them*?' We want the good rewarded and the bad punished. And yet, when we look around, it's clear this often doesn't happen. That can be immensely depressing and frustrating.

Of course, if you believe in a God who will see all wrongs righted and all virtue rewarded, then you believe that eventually, somehow – perhaps in the next life, if not in this life – justice *will* be done. That's a comforting thought. However, we then face another puzzle: the puzzle of explaining *why* a just God would allow the good to suffer so awfully in this life. How could a God who created a world that inflicts such horrific pain and suffering conceivably be *just*? This, of course, is one popular reason for rejecting belief in such a God. Many atheists believe the suffering of the good and the innocent shows that, even if there's *some* sort of intelligence in control of the universe, it's not particularly benevolent or just.

Might heaven offer a solution to this problem? If heaven exists, and the good get to go there, won't any suffering they experience in this life be more than adequately compensated for in the next? In which case, justice *will* ultimately be done.

But on closer examination, it's not clear how heaven succeeds in squaring the existence of a just and loving God with the depth of suffering good folk are forced to endure. The members of the Bullingdon Club – an elite, all-male dining club at the University of Oxford that boasts many leading Members of Parliament as old members – would enjoy completely trashing restaurants after their meal. After turning the place to wreckage, they'd hand a bundle of notes over to the owner, saying, 'That should take care of it.' Even if the value of the money handed over was vastly more than the financial loss they had caused the owner, it's clear it wouldn't have the effect of righting the wrong that had been done. Nor would it make their behaviour morally permissible. Mere compensation doesn't wipe the moral slate clean. Heaven may offer compensation to those who have been forced to suffer appallingly in the world that God, if He exists, has forced them to inhabit. But that compensation wouldn't justify God's causing or allowing that suffering in the first place.

Might there be a good reason for God to allow the good to suffer awfully? Those who believe in God believe there is such a reason, whether or not we happen to know what it is. 'Perhaps,' some say, 'it's just *beyond our ability to figure out*. After all, we are mere humans. There will, inevitably, be much we cannot understand.'

Perhaps the right attitude to have towards suffering is to try, as best we can, to reduce it. We have, very recently, brought down childhood mortality rates, allowing children who would, in almost any other generation of humans, have died, to flourish instead.[44] We have developed anaesthetics so that our suffering is significantly reduced.

28. Why don't I appreciate what I have?

▶ Result

We're all striving to obtain goals. There are material possessions we want: more money, that fancy car, a nicer house. We also strive after that new relationship, to have children, to get a higher status job, to swim with dolphins, and other non-material goods. When we've achieved our goal, we often feel happy for a while. Unfortunately, we humans tend to become habituated to whatever we've gained, and often find that, after a short while, we're no happier than we were before. Those who've just achieved a big sporting achievement or a lottery win enjoy an emotional rush, but then find that it doesn't last long.

To retain our elevated level of happiness we focus our attention on new goals; goals which, when achieved, deliver a new 'hit' of happiness, but one that is again often short-lived, leaving us thirsting for more. This endless cycle into which we humans often become trapped is called the *hedonic treadmill*. Those stuck on a physical treadmill have to keep walking or running just to stay where they are. The psychologist Michael Eysenck suggests that the pursuit of happiness places us on a similar treadmill: we have to keep striving just to stay where we are, happiness-wise.

The thought that the desire for happiness can place us on a treadmill or, the equine equivalent, a horse-mill is fairly old. It's attributed, for example, to the philosopher St Augustine, who is quoted as saying: 'A true saying it is, *Desire hath no rest*, is infinite in itself, endless, and as one calls it, a perpetual rack, or horse-mill.'[45]

There's an upside to our tendency to revert to whatever levels of happiness we had before a major happiness-affecting event occurred. If something happens that makes you deeply *un*happy – losing a job, say, or even losing a limb – you'll also tend to revert to your previous level of happiness after a few months. In a famous study published in 1987, 'Lottery Winners And Accident Victims: Is Happiness Relative?', psychologists Brickmann, Coates, and Janoff-Bulman found that while lottery winners were immediately very happy and those who had lost a limb immediately very sad, the levels of happiness of the two groups were about the same again after just a few months.

So how do we escape the hedonic treadmill? How do we achieve a more lasting form of happiness? In his

Why don't I appreciate what I have?

2013 TED talk 'The How and Why of Effective Altruism', Australian philosopher Peter Singer suggests that *altruism* offers us an escape hatch:

> You work hard to get money. You spend that money on consumer goods, which you hope you will enjoy using. But then the money is gone. You have to work hard to get more, spend more, and maintain the same level of happiness. It is kind of a hedonic treadmill. You never get off and you never really feel satisfied. Becoming an effective altruist gives you that meaning and fulfilment, it enables you to have a solid basis for self-esteem in which you can feel your life was really worth living.

Our contemporary consumerist lifestyle, says Singer, is a trap. We're like the character of Sisyphus in Greek mythology, who was condemned to push a boulder to the top of a hill, only to watch it roll back down so that he must push it up again, over and over again, for eternity. Rather than endlessly seeking the short-term hit of a purchase now, only to have to find the money to get another hit once the first wears off, we can, Singer believes, achieve a much more lasting sense of satisfaction by helping others. He suggests we should engage in what's known as 'effective altruism': giving money in the most effective ways to help the poor and disadvantaged.

There's evidence that a more lasting form of happiness can be achieved by changing our lifestyles. In 'Why don't I enjoy life?' we looked at seven ways that, research suggests, can help us to improve our own levels of happiness. One of those ways is indeed to *help others*, just as Singer recommends. But there are other things we can do too. The last of the seven happiness-boosting techniques we examined was to focus on *gratitude*. By focusing on gratitude we remind ourselves both of what is good in our lives, and also of the fact that what's good in our lives is at least partly out of our own control. We may be grateful to – and thereby come to feel a closer connection to – other people, to the world, and perhaps even to some sort of higher power.

A ten-week study compared a group that wrote about things for which they were grateful with a group that wrote about things that displeased or irritated them.[46] The study found that the first group became more optimistic and felt better about their lives. Interestingly, the first group also exercised more and saw doctors less than the second. Keeping a gratitude journal, by writing things down or perhaps just by telling friends and family, is one way that we can help ourselves both feel happier and appreciate what we have.

▷ Result

When people ask 'What are you doing with your life?' it's sometimes a veiled criticism. If an aunt asks it of a niece, for example, the aunt might well be implying the youngster is currently *wasting* her life. What the aunt is really asking is, in effect: 'Why aren't you getting on with *the things that we expect of you*, like building a successful career, getting married, and having children?' The aunt is letting the niece know that the niece is, from the aunt's perspective at least, a bit of a let-down.

When we ask ourselves this same question, it's often because we're feeling dissatisfied with ourselves. We may feel we're wasting our lives and letting ourselves down.

There's no doubt some people do waste their lives, or at least parts of their lives. There's also no doubt we can sometimes get 'stuck', finding ourselves trapped in a dull, monotonous routine, and failing to make any progress towards goals that are important to us. We can also be unsure about what our goals should be. Should we aim for something fairly conventional: a good career and a happy marriage, say? Or should we be setting our sights on something else?

I'm not going to offer any advice here on what your goals should be. However, I will warn against what I call 'The Curse of The Grand Narrative'. Humans love a good story – a plot with a satisfying narrative arc. We enjoy hearing tales of villains defeated, of heroes who prevail, of obstacles overcome. We like a story with a beginning, middle, and a satisfying resolution.

We often edit our own lives and the lives of those around us to try to make them conform to this narrative arc. Details are included and other features omitted in order to produce an engaging yarn. Biographies and biopics often do this. So do obituaries. And, of course, we do it to our own lives in those round robin letters some of us send each other at Christmas time.

The trouble is, many lives, when looked at in the round, don't live up to the expectation of a Grand Narrative. Real lives are typically messy and chaotic. They have to be heavily edited and redacted to give them anything like the shape of a pleasing plot. Consequently, if I compare the reality of my own life with what I read in round robins and see in biopics, I may well feel my own life is second-rate. I may be disappointed that my life has failed the test of being a Big Story.

Comparing our own lives with such largely mythical Grand Narratives is surely a mistake. We can lead good, worthwhile lives, even if they're not particularly epic or anecdote-rich. Someone who, from cradle to grave, has selflessly worked in small, quiet ways to improve the lives of those around them may have lived an exceptionally worthwhile life, despite the fact that their life would make for an *extremely* tedious biopic. By all means ask, 'What am I doing with my life?', but don't make the mistake of thinking that, unless your life takes the form of a Grand Narrative, it's a life wasted.

Of course, asking 'What am I doing with my life?' is the sort of question philosophers encourage us to ask ourselves. One of the most famous philosophy quotes is from Plato's *Apology*, in which Socrates says: 'the unexamined life is not worth living.' According to Plato's Socrates, if you don't ask yourself some penetrating philosophical questions about what you are, and should be, doing with your life, then your life is a *waste of time*. But then, if Socrates is right, by asking yourself, 'What am I doing with my life?' you're at least taking a step in the direction of making your life worthwhile!

But is Socrates right? In fact, isn't he, in effect, condemning all those who don't engage in philosophical reflection about their own existence as living worthless lives? Of course, as I'm a philosopher, you would expect me to be in favour of getting people to think philosophically. And I do think it's good for us. There's evidence that people raised to reflect on philosophical and moral questions – including how they should live – and apply their own intelligence and judgement, do benefit from it. However, I doubt engaging in such intellectual activity is the *only* way to lead a worthwhile life. Are the lives of people who work selflessly and effectively to help others, but who never intellectually reflect on what they do, lives not worth living? Is the life of someone who, because of a cognitive impairment, is unable to engage in such intellectual activity a life *not worth living*? That's a very dark and disturbing suggestion.

30. Did I make the right decision?

▶ Result

Here follows a confession. I'm prone to dwelling on the decisions I've made. I replay what I have said and done, asking myself: 'Was that the best thing to do? Perhaps I should have done the other thing?' Sometimes this somewhat obsessive, backward-looking tendency can become a serious distraction, drawing my attention away from what's going on right now and what's happening next.

Sometimes I go further: I don't just question whether I did the right thing, I judge that I did the *wrong* thing. I regret what I did and perhaps desperately wish I could go back and do things differently. Sometimes I'm overcome with remorse.

Is this a healthy thing to do? Some would advise me that what's done is done. The past can't be altered. So there's really *no point* in my looking back and questioning, even regretting, what I did. I should not focus on what I *can't* change – the past – but on what I *can* change: the present and the future.

That we should try to live life with no regrets was recommended by the philosopher Nietzsche. Nietzsche says: 'My recipe for greatness in a human being is *amor fati*'.[47] *Amor fati* is Latin for 'love of one's fate'. There is no point regretting, or indeed feeling remorse, for what we've done. For what is done can't be altered. Indeed, Nietzsche adds that to feel remorse for what you have done is to add 'to the first act of stupidity a second'.

Asking ourselves whether we did the right thing – and perhaps regretting what we did – comes naturally to us. It's part of the human condition. But why? Why have we evolved to mull over what can't be changed if doing so can be of no benefit to us?

The answer, of course, is that it *can* benefit us. While we can't change the past, we can learn from it. Those who look back at what they have done and the mistakes they have made are much better placed to avoid making those same mistakes again. Our tendency to replay in our heads episodes in which we have been involved, asking ourselves, 'Did I do the right thing then, and then … ?' can be to our advantage.

Perhaps the Stoics got it right on backward-looking soul-searching and regret? The Stoic philosophers Seneca, Epictetus, and Marcus Aurelius believed that negative emotions such as regret are unhelpful and should be avoided. The past cannot be altered, and so, thought the Stoics, we should not dwell on it emotionally, plagued by feelings of remorse about what can't be undone. However, as the philosopher Massimo Pigliucci points out,[48] that's not to say the Stoics thought that looking back *as such* is a mistake. By looking back, we can learn from the mistakes we've made. In fact, the Stoic Seneca, in his work *On Anger*, very much *encourages* us to look back at the end of each day and examine what we have done:

> The spirit ought to be brought up for examination daily. It was the custom of Sextius when the day was over, and he had betaken himself to rest, to inquire of his spirit: 'What bad habit of yours have you cured today? What vice have you checked? In what respect are you better?'... What can be more admirable than this fashion of discussing the whole of the day's events?[49]

Looking back and asking, 'Did I make the right decision?' can be a valuable exercise, say the Stoics. The mistake is to then allow negative emotions to start bubbling up so that we become distraught at what we've done. Those emotions are unhelpful and are not required for you to learn from your mistakes.

Result

'It's a hard-knock life!' sings Little Orphan Annie.
And it really is for many of us.

Why is life hard? Well, *why wouldn't it be?* Life is generally pretty hard for most sentient creatures on the face of this planet. Anyone who has watched a few nature documentaries will know that for most living things life is a desperate struggle for existence. Living things are often at constant risk of starvation, of physical attack by competitors and predators, and countless other threats. Only the toughest survive. The philosopher Thomas Hobbes (1588– 1679) famously argues that for someone living in a 'state of nature' outside of society, life would be 'solitary, poor, nasty, brutish, and short'. By living together within a society governed by laws and a state with the power to enforce those laws, we can at least live our lives in relative safety, confident that we're unlikely to be murdered in our beds.

True, for most contemporary Westerners life is much less hard than in the past, when the knocks were even harder. We were recently far more vulnerable to illness, pain, and abuse by others than we are today. Scientific, moral, and political advances have made our lives far more tolerable. Still, even today, most lives involve some degree of tragedy, and indeed many are filled with a great deal of it.

Given that life is hard, how do we cope? Perhaps part of the solution lies in managing our expectations. We often shield the brutal character of adult life from our children, coddling them in lullabies and lies. We tell them stories with happy endings. We insist that whatever they create is wonderful – 'That's beautiful, darling!', 'Oh, how lovely, we must put it on the fridge!' – no matter how hideous their scrawls or tuneless their singing. We also tell them that they can be whatever they want to be when they grow up. As a result, reaching adulthood can be a shock to the system. That tone-deaf kid, told that they could be whatever they wanted by the doting parent who praised their tuneless singing, is going to bitterly disappointed when they come up against reality. The hard knocks of disappointment will feel even harder.

If unrealistic expectations make things worse, shouldn't we work on managing those expectations? This suggestion lies at the heart of the philosophy of the Stoics, whom we have already discussed in 'Why am I angry all the time?', page 133, and 'Did I make the right decision?', page 163. The Stoics recommend we *manage our expectations* so as not to suffer disappointment when things don't go to plan.

When Little Orphan Annie suffers disappointment, she optimistically sings: 'The sun will come out tomorrow!' The Stoics say: that is *not* a helpful attitude. Actually, the sun may well not come out tomorrow. In fact, you should *expect* it not to come out tomorrow, because then, when it doesn't come out, you won't feel nearly so bad. Optimism and hope are your enemy, not your friend. As the Stoic Seneca puts it: 'Misfortune weighs most heavily on those who expect nothing but good fortune.'

One of the techniques recommended by the Stoics is called *premeditatio malorum* (it has more recently been dubbed *negative visualisation*). Suppose you are the owner of a shiny new bicycle. The Stoics suggest you should remind yourself that bikes are often stolen or damaged, that shiny new things soon tarnish, and so on. That way, if and when something bad happens to your bike, you won't be nearly so deflated and will be better prepared for the loss. Focusing on the potential loss of your bike brings another benefit too: you're more likely to appreciate your lovely bike while you still have it.

The Stoics recommend that we apply the technique of *premeditatio malorum* to everything we value highly. We should consider losing our loved ones, losing our health, losing all our possessions, and so on. In that way, we'll be better prepared for the hard knocks when they inevitably come.

It's important to remember, however, that what the Stoics recommend is *not* that we develop an attitude of permanent deep, Eeyore-like gloominess. The idea is not that we make ourselves so glum that, when something bad happens, we haven't got much further to fall emotionally. *Premeditatio malorum* is an *intellectual* exercise designed to help us develop realistic expectations and be prepared for bad things that will happen, not an *emotional* exercise designed to make us feel gloomy. The aim is to make ourselves happier, not sadder.

▷ Result

'Peter Singer Says You Are A Bad Person' says
the title of an article in *Philosophy Now* magazine. Peter
Singer is one of the world's foremost moral philosophers,
so I guess if Peter Singer does say you're a bad person
(and I am not sure he would say that, to be honest), then
it's worth taking the suggestion seriously.

Many people have a pretty negative view of humanity.
In 'Am I going to hell?' we saw that, according to some
religious believers, we're all so *very* bad that, unless we
believe in God – and perhaps also the salvation offered by
Jesus – we *deserve* hell.

That's certainly not Singer's view. However, it's true
that he thinks very many of us are *behaving* in a pretty
bad way. To see why, consider one of his philosophical
thought experiments: suppose you see a child drowning
in a pool. You alone can save the child, but only by

wading in and ruining your *very* expensive new suit. Obviously, the right thing to do is to save that child, the cost of the suit be damned. But now consider an analogous case: children in far-off lands that will die soon unless money is provided to buy them food and medical care. Most of us think that while it's good to save those children, we don't have a moral *obligation* to hand over large amounts of cash to save them. But why not? Singer thinks you have as much of a moral duty to save the child starving far away as the child drowning in front of you. The mere physical distance of the child from you is not morally relevant.[50]

Of course, it's much easier for us to ignore the plight of someone who is far away than the drowning child right in front of us. But just because it's easier doesn't make it right.

Singer believes that we should all give a good chunk of our income to effective charities: 5 per cent if you earn more than $10,000 per year and 10 per cent if you earn more than $150,000 a year. Singer himself gives away 20 per cent of his income to charity. If Singer is right, then, morally speaking, most of us are failing *very badly indeed*. Our behaviour is as bad as that of the person who lets a child drown in order to keep his expensive new suit dry.

Of course, you may have had the excuse that you *didn't know* how morally bad your behaviour was. Still, if you're persuaded by Singer's argument, you don't have that excuse anymore.

But is Singer right? That's controversial. Some argue that one relevant difference between the drowning child in front of you and the starving child far away is that *only you* can save the former child, while very many others can save the latter child. That puts you under much less of a moral obligation to act in the second case.

However, as Singer points out, this objection fails to provide you with an adequate excuse. Even if there are others at the poolside who might also jump in and save that drowning child, that doesn't mean that you are then morally excused from doing so. Many Germans looked the other way when Nazi atrocities were being committed: that doesn't mean they're all individually excused.

Whether or not Singer is right about charitable giving, it's certainly worth remembering that there have been many occasions in the past when many of us have behaved in morally appalling ways, though we possibly didn't realise it. There have been times and places where most people thought it morally acceptable to own other human beings as slaves, to discriminate against people on the basis of the colour of their skin, to keep women in servitude, and so on. Perhaps we're in a similar situation: thinking we're good even while doing very bad things?

The question 'Am I a bad person?' is often asked by someone looking back and worrying about their own past behaviour. As I explain in 'Who am I?', our behaviour is often a better guide to our *character* than is introspection and navel-gazing. There's no doubt that some of us *really are* bad people. We may have redeeming qualities, but on balance, we're much more bad than good, and our behaviour reveals that. On the other hand, some of us are clearly overly self-critical, focused on our own faults and forgetting about what good we have done. We're our own harshest critics. It's often difficult to make a reliable assessment of how good or bad we really are.

Are we *stuck* with how good or bad we are? It may be that some of us are born with, if not original sin, then genes that makes us more susceptible to rage and violence. One Finnish study found that criminals convicted of ten or more violent crimes were far more likely to carry variants in two genes than non-violent criminals. They believe the research indicated that 5 per cent to 10 per cent of all severe violent crime in Finland could be attributed to these genetic variants.[51]

Still, we're not slaves to our genes. Professor Simon Baron-Cohen, Professor of Developmental Psychopathology at the University of Cambridge, says that our behaviour is not more than 50 per cent determined by genetics. Indeed, the genetic variants that Finnish research linked to violent behaviour are pretty common. Many of us (one paper says 40 per cent of us) carry those genes, yet most of those carrying them don't end up violent criminals.[52] Our genes may give us behavioural susceptibilities, but we're not their puppets. We're *not* genetically 'born bad'.

33. What if I fail?

▶ Result

Johannes Haushofer, a professor at Princeton, recently published his 'CV of Failures', about which he says: 'This darn CV of Failures has received way more attention than my entire body of academic work.'[53] The CV lists every one of Haushofer's career failures. All the papers Haushofer failed to get published, all the positions he applied for but failed to get, all the funding bodies that rejected his applications are included. Haushofer says, 'Most of what I try fails, but these failures are often invisible, while the successes are visible. I have noticed that this sometimes gives others the impression that most things work out for me.' The truth, however, is that Haushofer failed *a lot*. Just like most successful people. Those who succeed have usually fallen many, *many* times along the way.

As Haushofer reminds us, it's easy to forget that failure is a necessary and important part of life. I know from my own experience that much of what I have attempted has not come off. That's the inevitable price I've paid for the success I've enjoyed. In fact, what success I have had has often been *built on* my failures. I've learnt from my mistakes.

Feeling like a failure is part of the human condition. Even the most successful people often feel they're failures. Paul McCartney, one of the world's most successful musicians, said in an interview, 'No matter how accomplished you get – and I know a lot of people who are very accomplished – you feel that everyone is doing better than you, that it's easier for them.'[54] If McCartney feels like a failure, then you can be forgiven for feeling the same way.

These feelings can be destructive. First of all, they may lead us to despair and so not even to try. True enough, if you don't try, you're guaranteed not to fail. But then you're guaranteed not to succeed either. Second, experience of repeated failure may lead us to give up *too soon*. We may try hard, but then quickly become dispirited when the rejection letters start dropping onto the doormat. Yes, it's important to acknowledge when something *really is* unattainable: a seven-foot-tall person is never going to ride the winner in the Epsom Derby no matter how hard they try. But on the other hand, many give up just a few hurdles in. Persistence is essential. Successful people are those who just doggedly keep going, despite racking up numerous failures along the way.

Elsewhere in this book I have looked at the philosophy of the Stoics, who encourage us to manage our expectations. They note that life inevitably throws many disasters at us. These will have a far more damaging effect on us if they're unexpected. So expect them. The Stoics would presumably say the same about failure: let's *expect* failure, so that, when we inevitably do fail, we're better able to cope with it.

However, *expecting* failure – indeed, planning for failure – is not the same as *focusing* on failure. I once got some tuition in mountain biking down narrow trails between potentially dangerous obstacles like boulders and trees. The advice I was given was: *never focus your attention on the obstacles*. Stare at that tree ahead of you, and you're much more likely to crash into it. Focus instead on the trail. Yes, be aware of the obstacle, and know what you'll do if things go wrong. But don't stare at the obstacle.

I suspect the more general moral here – that we should not focus our attention on our actual and potential failures – is valuable. Research suggests that failure breeds failure. One study found that monkeys that succeeded on a first trial did much better on subsequent trials, while those who made mistakes then went on to do no better than chance.[55]

But then isn't the Stoic thought that we should contemplate bad things happening to us in future – what the Roman Stoics called *premeditatio malorum* (see page 169) – in order to better manage our expectations is, in one important respect, counter-productive? Positive visualisation – seeing yourself successfully score that goal, make that hard climbing move, or throw that javelin a very long way – is one of the key techniques of sports psychology. It appears that imagining yourself succeeding makes it more likely you'll succeed. Conversely, it seems plausible that *imagining yourself failing makes failure more likely*. So while the Stoics may be right that it's a good idea to imagine bad things *entirely out of our control* happening to us, perhaps it's less helpful to imagine ourselves failing?

Perhaps the right way to approach failure is not to expect it or imagine it, but just to plan thoroughly for it. That way, we'll be more likely to cope with failure calmly and constructively when it happens.

34. Am I a psychopath?

Result

Psychopaths are fascinating: the subject of innumerable films and books. Characteristics of psychopathy include a lack of empathetic emotional response. An event that would bring most of us to tears, such as the loss of a close family member, may leave a psychopath strangely unmoved. In an online forum, Athena Walker, who describes herself as a diagnosed psychopath, says that:

> [I]t was very apparent that I was quite different than those around me. I could tell this from an early age, as soon as I was aware of other peoples' actions not matching my own. I didn't feel as they felt and that was obvious.[56]

And yet, because psychopaths know that tears and visible signs of distress are what's *expected* from someone who has just lost a close family member, they often learn to *act* as if they're distressed. Psychopaths typically wear a mask. Indeed, American psychologist Hervey Cleckley's (1903–1984) classic text on psychopaths is called *The Mask of Sanity*.

Other characteristics of psychopathy include fearlessness, impulsiveness, lack of guilt and remorse. Psychopaths are often very good at getting what they want through trickery and deceit. They often also demonstrate sadistic tendencies and may report having urges to hurt other people or animals. In the late nineteenth century, Jane Toppan, a nurse from Massachusetts, killed thirty-one people by administering lethal drugs. Adrian Raine, an expert on the physiological correlates of psychopathy, writes in his book *The Anatomy of Violence* that Toppan, a psychopath, reported that her greatest excitement was to watch the life being slowly sucked out of her patients. She said that watching the moment of their death gave her 'voluptuous delight'.

Clearly, psychopaths have the potential to cause the rest of us immense problems. But not all psychopaths are violent and dangerous. Some manage to lead fairly ordinary and successful lives, while suffering from the same lack of remorse, and so on. In fact, you've almost certainly met a psychopath. Psychopaths are said to constitute around 1 per cent of the population. Walk down a busy high street and you'll almost certainly walk past one or two, though you won't be able to identify them. Inwardly, psychopaths may be disturbingly different, but outwardly they're much like the rest of us.

Psychopaths are said to be drawn to certain professions. The Canadian psychologist Robert D. Hare – who devised the most common test of psychopathy (described below) – claims that while around 1 per cent of the population meet the clinical criteria for the condition, around 3 per cent to 4 per cent of those in senior business positions are clinically psychopaths. In fact, Hare says disgraced media magnate Robert Maxwell was probably a psychopath.

Psychopathy isn't considered a mental illness. Rather, it's classed as a type of personality disorder. In particular, psychopaths are not considered legally insane. They are thought to know the difference between right and wrong and to be fully aware of what they are doing. So, being diagnosed as a psychopath doesn't mean that you won't be held legally responsible for what you do (though you might be sent to a secure hospital rather than to prison).

What causes people to be psychopaths? The jury is out, but it seems that both nature and nurture play a role. It's well established that meeting the criteria for being a psychopath correlates with having certain unusual brain features, such as a smaller amygdala, which may explain why psychopaths are less empathetic (the amygdala is a small, almond-shaped part of the brain that plays a key role in processing emotions).

How can we tell if we're dealing with a psychopath? The standard diagnostic test was devised by psychologist Robert D. Hare and is called the Hare Psychopathy Checklist (or PCL-Revised).[57] The test involves twenty traits, which include, for example:

- glib and superficial charm
- grandiose (exaggeratedly high) estimation of self
- need for stimulation
- pathological lying
- cunning and manipulativeness
- lack of remorse or guilt
- shallow affect (superficial emotional responsiveness)
- callousness and lack of empathy.

When enough of these twenty traits are exhibited to a high enough degree, the subject meets the threshold for being a psychopath.

Of course, the temptation, when presented with a checklist like this, is to start checking those we know. 'Well, Uncle John *does* lie a lot, doesn't he? And can be quite callous ... My God! *He's a psychopath!*' Still, Hare is clear that his test should only be considered valid if conducted by a suitably qualified person under scientifically controlled conditions.

Are *you* a psychopath? Well, it's *possible*. Other things being equal, there's a 1 per cent chance that you are. But if this question is one that bothers you, then that actually makes it less likely you're a psychopath. Psychopaths aren't typically plagued by such worries and don't usually seek treatment. Of those diagnosed as psychopaths, the majority didn't present themselves to a medical or psychological professional for help. It's those affected by a psychopathic friend or family member who tend to seek assistance.

Psychopaths raise a number of interesting philosophical questions. We saw above that being a psychopath doesn't mean that a person is not criminally responsible for what they do. Psychopaths are considered morally responsible for the bad things they do: it's claimed that they fully understand that what they're doing is wrong.

But is that true? It depends, in part, on what philosophical view we hold about morality. The philosopher Kant believed that what's right and wrong is determined by *reason alone*. According to Kant, how we *feel* about, say, murder – our emotional response to it – is morally irrelevant so far as making a moral judgement is concerned. So, because psychopaths are as rational as the rest of us – they merely lack certain *emotional* responses – Kant's view would appear to have the consequence that a psychopath's deficiency in how they feel is no obstacle to them knowing what's right and wrong, just so long as their faculty of reason is working fine.

However, other philosophers, such as David Hume, insist that morality is ultimately rooted not in reason, but in our emotional responses. You won't find the wrongness of murder in the murder itself. Rather, it is revealed by looking inside ourselves and finding how we feel about murder. But then, if a psychopath lacks the kind of emotional responses we associate with a moral judgement – feelings of compassion, empathy, remorse, regret, and so on – perhaps they do, after all, suffer from a significant deficiency so far as moral understanding is concerned.

Of course, a psychopath can learn to *say* that repaying debts is 'right' and murder is 'wrong', in the same way that red–green colour blind people can learn to *say* that poppies are 'red' and grass is 'green'. Still, just as it's arguable that those who lack red and green colour experiences can't fully understand what 'red' and 'green' mean, some might say that those lacking the appropriate emotional experiences can't fully understand what 'right' and 'wrong' mean.

Even if Hume is wrong about morality being *entirely* rooted in our subjective feelings, it seems plausible that morality has at least *something* to do with how we feel. Consider two hospital visitors. One visits their sick colleague out of an entirely dispassionate assessment that this is what reason demands. However, they're entirely lacking in feelings of pity, empathy, compassion, and so on. Emotionally speaking, they don't care a jot about their ill associate. The other visits their colleague only because they're overwhelmed by such feelings towards their colleague. Which of these two visitors acts more morally? Kant would say that the second visitor doesn't act morally *at all*. If you're inclined to think the second person *does* act morally – perhaps even *more* morally than the first – that suggests you think that moral judgement and action have got at least *something* to do with our emotions.

35. Am I a good person?

▶ Result

<u>Before we consider the question of whether</u> *you* are a good person, let's state what should be obvious. Humanity does not fall cleanly into two boxes: the good and the bad. Dividing folk into the 'goodies' and the 'baddies' may be fun when we're kids playing a game, but we don't really divide up so easily. Most of us are neither heroes nor villains.

And of course, with the possible exception of Jesus, no human being is *perfectly* good. But then neither is anyone *entirely* bad. Goodness and badness lie at either end of a scale with us mortals distributed in between.

So what is a 'good person'? Presumably, if being a good person is to be achievable, it involves being *on balance* good. You need to be, say, at least two thirds of the way along the bad–to–good scale. Surely at least some of us qualify as good people, even if we're far from perfect. Are you one of them?

The fact that you're asking the question 'Am I a good person?' is a positive sign. It suggests you're concerned about morality and doing the right thing, and that you'd *like* to be a good person. Those who don't much care about whether they're good or bad, morally speaking, are far more likely to be found towards the bad end of the scale. So, if we can rule out your being one of them, that raises the probability you're a good person.

Still, plenty of people who care very much about doing the right thing fail to be good people. Among the most dramatic examples of people convinced they're doing the right thing, while clearly doing the wrong, are various misguided religious and political zealots, cultists, and crusaders. Some True Believers torture, maim, and kill even while thinking of themselves as 'good people'. They believe, wrongly, that engaging in such appalling behaviour is what's morally required of them. These folk are well intentioned. They *want* to do good, they *aim* to do good, and indeed they *think* they're doing good. But they're not good people.

Even the intention to do something that, as a matter of fact, *really is* good is not enough to make you a good person no matter how sincere your intention may be. Suppose I sincerely promise to return the car you lent me, saying, 'I really, *really* will return your car tonight, I *swear!*' and I mean that in all sincerity. If I then fail to return it because I am lazy or have taken a shine to the car, that's pretty good evidence I'm not a good person. A good person is a person of *good character*. And a person of good character is someone you can rely on to *behave* well even under challenging circumstances. They are people that can be trusted to do the right thing even when boredom, fatigue, or temptation set in.

Notice that having a good character is not just about doing things that happen to be good. A greedy, self-serving tycoon who, in trying to make himself more money, invests in a project that actually does a great deal of good may leave the world a substantially better place. Still, despite his good works, that tycoon is not a good person. The good outcome was a happy accident. It wasn't intended. So it seems that *intending* to do good is a requirement for being a good person, even if good intentions *alone* aren't enough to guarantee you're good.

So, are you a good person? Suppose you aim to do good, and fairly reliably achieve it. Is *that* enough to make you a good person?

Perhaps even that's not enough. The twentieth century provides dramatic examples of how ordinary human beings who have lived decent lives – who can usually be trusted to be honest, pay their debts, avoid stealing, and show kindness to strangers – can allow, and in some cases facilitate, moral horror. From the killing fields of Cambodia to Mao's China, to Stalin's Russia, to

Nazi Germany, we find people whom we might well have judged to be 'good people' on their previous track record suddenly behaving in an appalling fashion.

Interestingly, research has been done into the backgrounds of those who did behave well when unspeakable horror began to unfold in front of them. For, example, there's been research into the backgrounds of those who rescued Jews during the Holocaust. What was it about them that made them do the right thing even in the most extreme circumstances? The philosopher Jonathan Glover writes:

> If you look at the people who shelter Jews under the Nazis, you find a number of things about them. One is that they tended to have a different kind of upbringing from the average person, they tended to be brought up in a non-authoritarian way, brought up to have sympathy with other people and to discuss things rather than just do what they were told.[58]

Pearl and Samuel Oliner also conducted research into the backgrounds of rescuers and non-rescuers. In their book *The Altruistic Personality*, they report that 'parents of rescuers depended significantly less on physical punishment and significantly more on reasoning'.[59]

So, supposing we want to raise good people – good citizens who will resist the slide into such moral catastrophes – the evidence suggests we would do well to raise citizens who are prepared to think for themselves and take responsibility for making their own moral judgements rather than handing it over to some external authority, be it their local priest, imam, or communist party official. I suggest that we should avoid raising *moral sheep*: people who may reliably do the right thing, but only because that's what they're told to do by some benevolent authority. A society made up of such individuals may be well behaved, with no litter in the streets and little crime. Still, its citizens will have little ability to resist authority if it now decides to lead them dangerously astray. They'll continue to obey the orders and follow the rules.

Is a society made up of such individuals intent on doing good, who believe that doing good involves following the dictates of their religious, political, or other authority – an authority that happens to be benign – a society made up of 'good people'? I'll let you decide. But it seems to me that, whether or not we should call this a society of 'good people', it's potentially a morally catastrophic situation.

36. Am I the same person I was twenty years ago?

> Result

Many philosophers have the irritating habit of responding to a question by saying, 'Well, it depends what you mean by ... ' Still, that probably is the right response here. Are you the same person you were twenty years ago? Well, it depends what you mean by *'the same'.*

Just getting clear about what we mean is often half the battle in philosophy. An *awful* lot of philosophical trouble is caused by our not being sufficiently clear about what words mean. Here's an example.

Back in Ancient Greece, a philosopher called Heraclitus asked: 'Can I jump in the same river twice?' We don't know exactly what Heraclitus was driving at, but it's possible he thought you couldn't jump in the same river twice, and for the following reason.

Suppose you jump in the river at 1 p.m. Then you climb out, and jump in a second time at 1.05 p.m.

195

During those five minutes the river will have changed in various ways. The water will have moved on, the mud will have moved about, and the reeds will have grown a tiny bit. So the river won't be the same. But if it's not the same river you jumped into, then *the number of rivers you have jumped into must be two, not one*. The first river has *disappeared* and been replaced by a second river!

That seems like an absurd conclusion. Almost everyone assumes you *can* jump in one and the same river twice over. So, should we accept this seemingly absurd conclusion, or is there something wrong with the argument for it?

Actually, there is something wrong with the argument. We unwittingly slid between two different meanings of the words 'the same'. Sure, when you jump in at 1.05 p.m., the river is not exactly 'the same' as it was before, in the sense that it has *changed in its qualities or properties*. The mud has shifted position and the water has moved along. But then we ended up concluding that one river had been switched for another – that the number of rivers is two. That's a different kind of 'sameness', called *numerical*, as opposed to *qualitative* sameness.

This is an important, but easily missed, difference in meaning. I could have two objects that were qualitatively the same but not numerically the same – two absolutely identical pens, for example.

Or I could have a single pen that last week was full of ink and today is empty – it has changed in its qualities. You can still have numerically *one and the same object* even though it is not qualitatively the same as it was before. If I dent my car, it's still my car. If I take a bite out of an apple, the apple doesn't cease to exist to be replaced by a brand new apple.

Because we kept using the words 'the same', we missed this switch in meaning, and so ended up drawing an absurd conclusion. It does *not* follow that if the river has changed qualitatively then it has changed numerically.

Once we're clearer about qualitative and numerical sameness, we're going to be much better placed to answer such questions as: Is this the same pen I had before? Is this the same dog I saw before? And also the question: Am I the same person as the person I see in this twenty-year-old photo?

Sure, you have changed a lot over twenty years. You've changed physically, of course. You have also changed psychologically: your store of memories is very different. So, you're obviously not *qualitatively* the same after twenty years. But it doesn't follow that you are not *numerically* one and the same person as the person in the photograph.

So what *makes* you one and the same person as that earlier individual? Why, when we look at you now and you in that old photograph, are we looking not at *two different* people, but at one and the same person? This is a famous philosophical puzzle. There's no consensus about how to answer it, but here are two leading philosophical theories.

I will call the first theory *the animal theory* as it says that what you are, essentially, is an animal, and so you necessarily go wherever that animal goes. The animal theory neatly explains why it's you that we're looking at in the twenty-year-old photo: it's the same human animal that we see. You've just got older, and perhaps also a bit taller, or fatter, or thinner, or whatever. The animal theory has its difficulties, however. If you've ever seen the film *Freaky Friday*, starring Lindsay Lohan as a daughter and Jamie Lee Curtis as her mother, you'll know the plot involves them switching bodies after a magical encounter with a fortune cookie. All the daughter's personality traits, memories, and other psychological features get switched over to her mother's body, and vice versa. *Voilà*! According to the film, *they wake up in different bodies*! Only, according to the animal theory, they *don't* switch bodies. If it's the same animal in the daughter's bed next morning, then it's the daughter. Yes, the daughter has become psychologically *exactly like* her mother. But that's not the mother in the daughter's bed. It's still the daughter. This just doesn't strike us as the right verdict, though: surely the daughter has switched animal bodies with her mum. So the animal theory seems counter-intuitive when we consider this sort of 'body swap' case.

The other leading alternative theory – I'll call it the *psychological property theory* – says you go wherever the right memories and various other psychological properties, go. So, if those properties were to switch animal bodies, then so would you. The psychology theory seems to give the right verdict when we consider whether you are the person in that twenty-year-old photo. It's you, because you share the right kind of memories and other psychological features with that earlier person (sure, you may have lost some memories and gained some new ones over twenty years, but there are still innumerable overlapping memories linking you back to that earlier person). Unlike the animal theory, the psychological property theory gives intuitively the right verdict on *Freaky Friday*: the mother and daughter really do swap bodies as the relevant psychological properties get switched around, and the person goes where the properties go.

However, the psychological property theory faces a problem of its own. According to the theory, there's no reason in principle why there couldn't be two of you. Suppose a sort of high-tech copying device is created. Put a teapot inside, press the button, and two exactly similar teapots come out. The original teapot is now accompanied by its perfect duplicate.

Now suppose we put *you* in the device. Out pop two of you, at least according to the psychological property theory. Except there can't be two of you. Sure, both the people who step out are *exactly like* you – even psychologically. They're currently *qualitatively* the same as each other and also identical with the person – the you – who stepped in. But they can't both be *numerically* identical with the person who stepped in, as they would then be *numerically identical with each other*, which they're not (there are definitely two people now standing there, not one). So, as the psychological property theory entails both these later individuals *are* you, it must be wrong.

In fact, in this 'reduplication' scenario, notice that it's the animal theory that seems to give the right verdict. Only one of the two people who step out of the machine is you: the one that is *the same animal* that stepped in. The other person is a mere *copy* of you, not you.

So what makes it *you* that we see in that twenty-year-old photo of you? There's no philosophical consensus about that.

37. Why do I push people away?

▶ Result

Why do we push others away? For many different reasons. One of the more abstract reasons is articulated by the French philosopher Jean-Paul Sartre, often quoted as saying: 'Hell is other people.' The famous phrase is actually uttered by a character in Sartre's play *No Exit*, in which three people find themselves in hell. Only, hell is not what they expected. There's no torture chamber or lake of fire. It's just the three of them in a drawing room. Slowly, they figure out that they are to supply their *own* torture by being trapped in each other's company for eternity. Eventually, one of them finally realises the truth: there is no need for red hot pokers. Hell is other people.

But why should being trapped in the company of others be a kind of hell? Sartre later explained in some production notes for *No Exit* that he didn't mean everyone is always awful or that our relations with others are always poisoned. Rather, Sartre says that:

> ... if relations with someone else are twisted, vitiated, then that other person can only be hell. Why? Because ... when we think about ourselves, when we try to know ourselves ... we use the knowledge of us which other people already have. We judge ourselves with the means other people have and have given us for judging ourselves.[60]

Sartre seems to be making a point about our judgement of ourselves: that we can know ourselves only by means of the *mirror provided by others*. When that mirror is twisted, showing us a distorted and deformed version of ourselves, then being compelled to look endlessly at that reflection becomes unbearable.

So *one* reason why we may push people away is that they reflect back at us a version of ourselves that we find distorted and disturbing. Who wants to look in a mirror like that?

Clearly, we fear the negative judgement of others. And, of course, we also fear other potentially negative consequences of making ourselves emotionally vulnerable to others. Indeed, that's a standard explanation for why someone tends to push others away. A psychotherapist might well explain the difficulties a person may have with starting close relationships now as a consequence of their earlier painful rejection – by a parent, say. It can be hard to trust others if the track record of letting others emotionally enter your life has been catastrophic, or even just persistently disappointing. Yet most of us do still want such close relationships. As a result, we may find ourselves torn. When others come knocking, we open the door, but then we panic and quickly slam it shut again. If that's the situation you find yourself in, you need to figure out and deal with what's causing you to slam the door. A therapist might be able to help you.

Another reason we may want to be alone is that, frankly, for many of us, social encounters can be hard work. An hour or two having to make conversation is exhausting. Eventually, we may just want some time to ourselves. This can be true even when it comes to people close to us. While the company of other humans can be marvellous, it can also be boring, irritating, and a distraction.

Some believe a little solitude is helpful if we want to achieve insight – particularly into ourselves. Living as a hermit, at least for a while, is widely supposed to offer us a spiritual and/or intellectual springboard. Jesus spent forty days and nights living alone in the desert. The philosopher Ludwig Wittgenstein lived for a period of time alone in a secluded hut in Skjolden: a beautiful mountainous spot at the end of a Norwegian fjord. Wittgenstein later said of his time in Norway: '[I]t seems to me that I had given birth to new movements of thought within me.' Friedrich Nietzsche's novel *Thus Spoke Zarathustra* has his fictional hermit Zarathustra emerge like Moses descending from the mountain to reveal a new, life-enhancing philosophy to the world.

So, there does appear to be value for at least some of us in quieting the noise, and ridding ourselves of distractions, including being with others. Taking some time for yourself might not result in you developing a radical new philosophy. But still, pushing others away for a while can help bring about useful inner change.

38. How do I move on?

 Result

<u>Sometimes we find ourselves in a bad place as a</u> result of bereavement, a relationship ending, or some other calamity. These traumatic experiences may affect us so strongly that we find ourselves stuck, unable to get on with our lives. When grief strikes so catastrophically, how can we get ourselves unstuck?

I have mentioned the Stoic philosophers before, and hope I'll be forgiven for mentioning them again, as they are unsurpassed as philosophers when it comes to offering advice for dealing with life's troubles. As we have seen – in 'Why am I angry all the time?', 'What if I fail?', and 'Why is life so hard?' – the Stoics remind us that what we value most in life is always temporary. The way to deal with their loss is to develop an outlook that will emotionally prepare you for when disaster strikes. The Stoic Epictetus recommends that:

At the times when you are delighted with a thing, place before yourself the contrary appearances. What harm is it while you are kissing your child to say with a lisping voice, 'Tomorrow you will die'; and to a friend also, 'Tomorrow you will go away or I shall, and never shall we see one another again'? ... we ought not to hesitate to utter them in order to protect ourselves against the things.[61]

But what if disaster has already struck? What can we do to help ourselves then?

The Stoics remind us that if the loss is irrevocable – if a loved one has died, or clearly left us for a new relationship, never to return – there's no point causing ourselves to be unhappy by emotionally dwelling on it. The past can't be changed. They recommend that we root out both fear of future suffering, and also the pointless recollection of past suffering, in so far as both cause us entirely pointless distress.

So should our advice to others when they're consumed with grief be: pull your socks up and *stop dwelling*? Obviously, that would be not only ridiculously insensitive, but probably also counter-productive. The Stoics weren't foolish enough to suppose that we can turn off our emotions just like that. Being told to be rational and 'get a grip' immediately after tragedy has struck is likely only to make our suffering worse, as Seneca explains to his grieving mother:

> I knew that I must not oppose your grief during its first transports, lest my very attempts at consolation might irritate it, and add fuel to it: for in diseases, also, there is nothing more hurtful than medicine applied too soon. I waited, therefore, until it exhausted itself by its own violence, and being weakened by time, so that it was able to bear remedies, would allow itself to be handled and touched.[62]

So, don't be an insensitive oaf. However, once someone can start to think a little more clearly about their loss, it can be helpful to remind them that backward-looking self-torment is of no help to anyone.

That doesn't mean that revisiting past experiences has nothing to teach us. As we have seen, we can learn from our mistakes. If it was something stupid we did that forever drove our lover away, then reflecting in an *intellectual* way on our mistake can be a useful exercise. It's *emotionally* replaying over and over what can't now be undone that the Stoics say we should avoid.

Of course, it is one thing to recognise the wisdom in the Stoics' advice and say, 'Yes, I shouldn't do that'; it's quite another to internalise and be able to act on it.

Epictetus writes:

> ... practise what you have learnt. For it is not arguments that are wanting nowadays: no, the books of Stoics are full of them. What then is the one thing wanting? We want the man who will apply his arguments, and bear witness to them by action.[63]

How do we change ourselves in this more fundamental way, so that we don't just casually sign up to Stoic thoughts, but act on them? We must develop better *habits*. As the contemporary Stoic philosopher Massimo Pigliucci puts it in his book *How To Be A Stoic*: 'simply recognizing the truth of something is not enough: you need to practice it, over and over, until you develop a habit.'[64] So, get into the habit, perhaps once a day, of checking your own patterns of thought. Ask yourself such questions as: 'Are these emotions helping me or hindering me?' and: 'Am I pointlessly worrying about things I can do nothing about?' And regularly remind yourself, calmly and dispassionately, that things change, disasters happen, and nothing lasts forever.

39. Should I be allowed to say whatever I want?

 Result

Almost everyone in the West values free speech: the right to express our opinions without censorship or constraint. Free speech is considered one of the cornerstones of democracy. At the same time, almost everyone also agrees that there should be at least *some* restrictions on what we're allowed to say. If you go around libelling and slandering other people, you'll likely end up in court. If you make false claims in your advertising, you may be prosecuted. If you incite violence against a minority, or lie as a witness in a court of law, or reveal state secrets that put your nation's security at risk, then you also risk being locked up. There are many reasonable restrictions on what people can say, even in countries that proudly proclaim themselves to be 'free'.

So where should we draw the line between what can and can't be said? In particular, what speech should be banned, and why?

One of the most cited philosophers on this question is John Stuart Mill who, in his book *On Liberty* (published in 1859), provides a powerful defence of free speech. Mill offers four arguments for freedom of thought and expression, one of which is as follows.

No one should feel particularly confident in their own opinions, says Mill, if those opinions have not been exposed to critical scrutiny by others. History provides countless examples of authority figures who, convinced that they are right, have gagged dissenters who were actually correct. For example, the Catholic Church tried to prevent Galileo claiming the Earth moved. Yet Galileo was right. Mill argues that if we want to be justifiably confident in our beliefs, we should let them fight it out in the marketplace of ideas, not stifle dissent.

Still, even Mill argues that there are *some* circumstances in which speech can and should be restricted. In determining what those circumstances are Mill appeals to his 'Harm Principle'. The 'Harm Principle' says that the only purpose for which power can be rightfully exercised over any member of a civilised community, against his will, is to prevent harm to others. According to Mill, the state should leave us free to do our own thing – including to say whatever we like – *unless what we do causes harm to others*. At that point, the state can legitimately step in and restrain us.

Mill himself provides the following illustration. To claim that corn dealers starve the poor is acceptable in print, but not if shouted at an angry mob outside a corn dealer's door, given the violence that's likely to result. In those circumstances, yelling such things would be a dangerous abuse of free speech.

The Harm Principle sounds plausible. The state allows me to drive my car, but not in a way that endangers others. Similarly, the state allows me to say what I like, unless what I say is likely to harm others.

The devil, however, is in the detail. What, *exactly*, counts as 'harm'? Does only *physical* harm count – such as the physical injury caused by shouting 'Fire!' in a crowded theatre? What of financial harm, when someone lies about your products being dangerous, causing you to lose business? What about mental harm, such as that caused by persistent, bigoted name-calling and abuse? Shouldn't all this be included too?

It seems clear not *all* harms should be prevented. Suppose someone calls me a twit and I feel a little down as a result. I've suffered some slight mental harm. Should that person be arrested? Of course not. While Mill is not entirely clear what counts as a relevant harm, he discounts mere hurt feelings and mental discomfort. The fact my speech offends someone is never, according to Mill, a reason for the state to gag me.

Others disagree. They suppose that causing offence can be a justification for restricting speech. We don't allow people to wander around naked in public, despite the fact that no very substantial harm is done (the worst that usually results is that some onlookers feel a little uncomfortable and offended). But if we can justifiably restrict some behaviour – such as supermarket shopping in the nude – for no other reason than that many find it indecent and offensive, why can't we reasonably restrict offensive speech for the same reason?

The debate about free speech is largely defined by which harms and/or offences the state is justified in preventing. Take, for example, laws against blasphemy and bigotry. In many countries, blasphemy is illegal. The usual justification is that blasphemy is an insult to religion and offends many.

But why should religious beliefs get this special protection not afforded to other beliefs? Political beliefs can be lampooned and ridiculed. So why should lampooning and ridiculing religious beliefs be prohibited, if lampooning and ridiculing political beliefs is acceptable?

Suppose someone replies: because in a healthy democracy, political beliefs need to be open to severe criticism and even satire. But that wouldn't justify placing religious beliefs off-limits, because *religious beliefs are often highly political.* Consider, for example, religious beliefs about charitable giving, the role of women, the rights of gay people, the right to die, and the rights of unbelievers.

What about the supernatural focus of religious beliefs? Does that justify the state protecting them from mockery and ridicule? No. Plenty of supernatural beliefs, such as beliefs in ghosts, or psychic powers, aren't – and clearly shouldn't be – protected from ridicule. Nor is the fact that religious beliefs involve a passionate commitment, with people willing to die for their beliefs, what qualifies them for special protection. Many non-religious people are *also* prepared to die for their political beliefs, and have done so, yet their beliefs aren't considered off-limits. So, again, why should religious beliefs get privileged treatment?

In fact, on closer inspection, isn't the special 'respect' we're supposed to pay religious beliefs an historical anachronism – something we've got used to granting, but for no good reason? And isn't caving in to those who claim to be offended by such criticism or jokes at their religion's expense just going to encourage *more* offence-taking and demands for 'respect', with the result that free speech becomes seriously eroded? many would argue that blasphemy laws are an unjustifiable restriction on free speech.

Another area where speech is often restricted is where it fuels hatred, particularly against vulnerable minorities.

It's right that people are legally protected from facing torrents of abuse as they walk down the street because of their race, sexual orientation, particular religious belief, or disability. But then, what about, say, gay people being forced to hear religious people condemning the actively gay from street corners? Should the state permit that? Or what if members of the Dutch Reformed Church of South Africa loudly proclaimed on the High Street that anyone in a relationship with someone of a different race is a moral abomination? Is that permissible free speech, or an unacceptable expression of bigotry?

This issue is often presented as a clash of rights: the rights of religious people to express their religious beliefs vs. the rights of minorities not to be subjected to bigoted and hateful speech. However, if the religious have no special *extra* rights simply by virtue of being religious, why should they be exempt from the anti-discrimination legislation that applies to everyone else?

Of course, we do *sometimes* reasonably accommodate people whose beliefs are in tension with legislation or work requirements. For example, we don't force doctors who morally object to abortion to perform them (whether their objection is religious or not). But is it reasonable to exempt religious people from the laws that outlaw expressions of bigotry towards minorities? Should hoteliers be legally prevented from putting up signs saying 'No Irish', 'No blacks', 'No Catholics', 'No Jews', and 'No gays' unless their bigotry happens to be religiously rooted – in which case should the state say, 'Go right ahead'? That would be entirely unacceptable surely.

We've been focused on *legal* restrictions on free speech. But of course these aren't the only restrictions. In many Western countries, there is growing concern about free speech on campus and the practice of 'no platforming' speakers. In the UK, a speaker highly critical of Islam had her invitation to speak at a university student event withdrawn on the grounds that she was 'Islamophobic'. Speakers with views on gender have also been no-platformed on the grounds that they are, allegedly, bigoted against women or against transgender people. There's also the concern – expressed by, for example, Kenneth Stern, an initial drafter of the well-known International Holocaust Remembrance Alliance (IHRA) definition of anti-Semitism – that some accusations of anti-Semitism made on UK campuses against critics of Israel are 'McCarthyite' and are having a 'chilling' effect on free speech.

Can you say whatever you like? Obviously not. There are various legal restrictions on what you can say, even in the 'Land of the Free'. There are also social pressures on us to self-censor. Sometimes restrictions on free speech are reasonable, sometimes not. Deciding which restrictions are, and are not, reasonable is no easy task.

40. Would it be good to live forever?

There are various things we can do to prolong our lives. We can eat healthily and get plenty of exercise. In the future, technology may allow us to do a great deal more. Eventually, we may be able to turn off ageing, or acquire new bodies as our old bodies wear out, or perhaps even upload ourselves into robot or virtual bodies.

Most of us want more life than the amount we're usually allotted. But how much more life do we want? Would you want to go on ... *forever*?

Various religions promise followers eternal life. But how desirable is life without end? It depends in part on what sort of life it is. According to the Bible, the joys of heaven involve a great deal of singing God's praises, a prospect the author Mark Twain doesn't find terribly appealing:

Singing hymns and waving palm branches through all eternity is pretty when you hear about it in the pulpit, but it's as poor a way to put in valuable time as a body could contrive.[65]

Being in the company of God would no doubt be indescribably great. But wouldn't even that joy start to fade a bit after a few thousand years?

As we saw in 'Why don't I appreciate what I have?', page 155, it seems we human beings are constituted so that while something bad like losing a limb, or good like winning the lottery, can make us sadder or happier for a while, we fairly quickly adjust and return to roughly the same level of happiness that we had before. But if that's true, then it seems that in order to enjoy eternal, perpetual bliss in the company of God, something fairly radical is going to have to change – not only in our environment but also *in us* – if we're not to find even God a bit of a yawn.

What of an eternal *earthly* existence? Is that desirable? Wouldn't that eventually become boring? In the opera *The Makropulos Case* by Leoš Janáček (1854–1928), which is based on Karel Čapek's play of the same name, the central character, the opera singer Emilia Marty (formerly Elina Makropulos), is provided with an elixir by her father. The elixir will indefinitely extend Emilia's life if she continues to take it. She has now lived over three hundred years, yet still doesn't look a day over thirty. However,

Emilia has grown to find life unbearably dull. After seducing a baron, she reclines, completely indifferent to what she's just experienced. She laments that: 'In the end, it's the same, singing and silence.' Emilia refuses to take the elixir again, preferring to die.

In his celebrated paper 'The Makropulos Case: Reflections on The Tedium of Immortality', the English philosopher Bernard Williams (1929–2003) agrees that while dying too early is a bad thing, dying too late may also be a bad thing, and, as Elina Makropulos comes to recognise, being unable to die would actually be a curse. In which case, even if some form of Earth-bound immortality is technologically achievable, perhaps in the form of an elixir of life, or through our being uploaded in electronic form into robot or virtual bodies, it's debatable whether it's actually desirable.

Unless. What if we could be uploaded into a *virtual* environment that is perfectly suited us? It could provide endless novel stimulation. It could also improve us – educating us, constantly opening new doors to us – so that even if we became bored with one activity, there would be endless others we could take up. Poor Elina Makropulos may have become bored with sex and singing, but she did not have to continue as a singer. She might have become an explorer, a cellist, a surgeon, an architect, or a scientist. Equipped with virtual bodies, our horizons would be even less limited. We could change ourselves so that we could breathe under water or travel through space unaided. We could enjoy meeting an ever-expanding circle of fascinating people. And our environment needn't be limited to just this universe bound by its particular laws. We could even explore alternative, physically impossible realities.

Still, the worry persists: wouldn't even endless novelty get boring? Wouldn't novel experience after novel experience become a drag? Wouldn't we eventually feel trapped and bored by even an endless merry-go-round of delights?

Actually, I don't see why endless new stimulation is required to make life endlessly enjoyable. What most of us seem to enjoy is just *more of the same*. We like a bit of variety: in the food we eat, for example. But then we like that variety repeated: 'Great, it's Friday. Fish *again*!' But if that's how we're constituted – to enjoy routine – then I see no obvious reason why eternal life should inevitably become boring.

Even if some of us humans are put together in such a way that we require constant new delights in order to remain happy, we could rewire ourselves so that we don't. One obvious fix would be to limit our memories. Even if you've eaten a particularly exotic and exciting flavour of ice cream countless times before, you're not going to think, 'Oh, not *this* again', if you can't *remember* eating it before. The millionth taste will be as wonderful as the first.

In short, I'm not convinced eternal life must inevitably become tedious.

Q 41. Am I a narcissist?

 Result

In Book III of the Roman poet Ovid's (43 BC–C.AD 18) *Metamorphoses* – written in the first century BC – we meet Narcissus, a boy so beautiful that all the nymphs fall in love with him. When Narcissus bends down to drink water from a lake, he sees his own reflection for the first time. Narcissus becomes so entranced by his own beauty that he can't stop looking. Utterly captivated, he lies down. Eventually he dies.

Just like Narcissus, narcissists are consumed with self-love. They're so enamoured with themselves that it becomes a problem, just as it did for Narcissus. They may become so totally self-absorbed that they begin to lose touch with – and any appreciation of – anything beyond themselves. For the narcissist, life is all about 'Me, me, me!'

Westerners are often accused of increasing narcissism. When you look at social media, it's easy to see why. Rather than look at our reflections in a lake, we capture our images in selfies and gaze at them on screens. On a recent visit to an art gallery, I was struck by how uninterested people were in the actual paintings. They were primarily interested in taking selfies with the paintings functioning as backdrops. It was the portraits of themselves that most fascinated the visitors. We pout, we preen, we pose. And then we gaze, captivated by our own reflections.

Still, what's wrong with a bit of self-love? It's said that we can't love others unless we love ourselves. Whitney Houston sang 'The Greatest Love of All', reminding us of the importance of self-love. Perhaps it's no bad thing if we value ourselves highly. In fact, isn't it actually a *good* thing to love ourselves as much as we love those dearest to us?

Aristotle may have some insight to offer here. According to Aristotle, being a virtuous person is always a matter of balance. We must maintain what he calls the *golden mean*, which lies between two undesirable extremes. Finding the golden mean is the secret to leading a good and happy life.

Consider, for example, courage. Courage lies between two extremes. On the one hand there is cowardice: running away from any danger. On the other hand there's recklessness: running pointlessly into danger without a plan. Courage, the virtue, lies midway between these two undesirable poles.

Or consider being, on the one hand, excessively extravagant and generous, and, on the other, mean and penny-pinching. Again, as Aristotle's follower, the Islamic philosopher al-Ghazali (c. 1056–1111) points out, the virtuous person adopts a position midway between these two extremes:

> What is wanted is a balance between extravagance and miserliness through moderation, with the goal of distance between both extremes.[66]

The Italian philosopher–theologian St Thomas Aquinas (1225–1274), who was heavily influenced by Aristotle, and who became a huge influence on subsequent Christian thought, adopted Aristotle's view on virtue, arguing that:

> … evil consists in discordance from [the proper] rule or measure. Now this may happen either by their exceeding the measure or by their falling short of it[.] … Therefore it is evident that moral virtue observes the mean.[67]

Whether or not Aristotle, al-Ghazali, and Aquinas are right that virtue *always* involves finding a midpoint between two extremes, they may at least be right regarding self-love. On the one hand, there's the extreme of deficiency: an attitude of utter indifference or even contempt towards ourselves. Clearly, that is not a good state of affairs. On the other hand, there's the extreme narcissism: self-love taken to the point where it begins to damage our ability to lead a good life. Ideally, we must find a healthy balance between these two poles.

So, are *you* a narcissist? Hopefully, you are someone who loves yourself to a healthy degree. A deficiency in self-love is a bad thing (though Aristotle would add you should love the right things about yourself – your virtue, not your beautiful reflection in a mirror). But are you guilty of an excess of self-love? In particular, do you find that your selfies are becoming an obstacle to real life? Do you admire yourself to the point where you treat other people – even friends and family – as mere bit part players in a narrative that's all about, you, you, you? If so, then, yes, you may be guilty of narcissism.

A perfectionist is someone who strives for perfection. They may also demand perfection from others. But what's wrong with that?

Clearly, being a perfectionist can have downside. If you demand perfection of yourself, but given our human weaknesses and limitations, rarely if ever attain it, then you're likely to feel constantly disappointed in yourself. You might even suffer from low self-esteem or depression as a result.

If, as an employer or family member, you demand perfection from others and, being all too human, they too fall short, then your attitude is likely to make them feel bad about themselves. They will also come to resent your ludicrously high expectations.

Perfectionism has a further downside. It can result in a kind of paralysis. If I demand nothing less than perfection when looking for a new job, car, or life partner, and perfection is unattainable, then I'll have to do without. If every option is rejected as not good enough, I'll end up stuck with no life partner, no home, no car, and no job.

Yet being a perfectionist can have its advantages. True enough, if perfection is unattainable, the perfectionist will never achieve it. But still, by striving to seek perfection we may achieve far more than we might otherwise. Shoot for the stars, and you might at least reach the Moon. Those who are happy to settle for the so-so, on the other hand, are unlikely to achieve much more than the so-so.

In *The Impossibility of Perfection: Aristotle, Feminism, and the Complexities of Ethics*), philosopher Michael Slote argues that perfection is unattainable. Why? Well, consider the perfect garden. The perfect garden may have a perfectly manicured green and weed-free lawn, perfectly formed roses, and each plant displayed to its best possible advantage. But what if not all of these things can be achieved simultaneously? What if displaying one plant to its best advantage inevitably means others must take second place? Then the perfect garden will be unachievable. Slote argues that, similarly, while both frankness and tact are virtues, a person cannot be both perfectly tactful *and* perfectly frank. Someone who is perfectly frank must inevitably be somewhat lacking in tact. But then no one can be a *perfectly virtuous person* exhibiting both perfect frankness *and* perfect tact.

Still, even if no one can, in reality, be, like Mary Poppins, 'practically perfect in *every* way', couldn't we in principle at least achieve a best possible *balance* of the various virtues? So shouldn't we at least aim for that?

Some argue that if perfection is unattainable, then there's no point trying to achieve it. However, others would say that's a pernicious philosophy. We will never entirely eradicate criminality, or racism, or poverty. But that's not a reason not to try to achieve zero criminality, racism, or poverty. And it's obviously not a reason to say, 'As criminality, racism, and poverty will always be with us, there's no point trying to tackle these things: let's focus our efforts on achieving something else.'

Perfection is often thought of in other-worldly terms. Plato famously observed that we have an idea of perfection, though never actually experience it. I have the idea of a perfect triangle, for example, but have never actually seen a perfect triangle. Any triangle I come across always falls short of perfection; for example, the sides will not be perfectly straight. So where did I get the idea of a perfect triangle? Plato suggests that you were, in a sense, born with it. You were exposed to true perfection – including the perfect triangle – before you were born. The reason you can recognise things as being triangles now is that you have this previous knowledge of the perfect, other-worldly exemplar with which you can now compare them. Plato called these perfect other-worldly entities the *Forms*. The realm of the Forms is the eternal unchanging reality from which the imperfect examples we see in this world derive their temporary, impermanent existence. (I say more about this in 'Is there more to life than this?' on page 243.)

So Plato agrees that while perfection exists, it is not achievable in this world. There's also a sense in which, if Plato is right, *we are all perfectionists*. For we all carry deep within us knowledge of perfection, and compare what we see around us with this dimly remembered perfection.

But is Plato right?

43. Is violence ever justified?

According to some, violence is *never* the answer, no matter how dire our predicament. Even if some mad axe man is threatening you and your family, and the only way to stop him is to shoot him dead, it's *still* wrong for you to resort to doing so.

Of course, this *absolute* prohibition on violence is widely dismissed as ludicrous. Most of us think that not only is it not wrong to resort to violence in such a dire situation, it would be *wrong not to resort to violence* if the alternative is that innocent people will be brutally murdered.

Still, there are some who take this extreme view. Some take it on biblical grounds. One of the Ten Commandments is: 'Thou shalt not kill.' Jesus famously said: 'But I say unto you, that ye resist not evil: but whosoever shall smite thee on thy right cheek, turn to him the other one also.'[68] And it's not just the religiously motivated who consider it wrong to respond to violence with violence. In Plato's dialogue the *Crito*, Socrates also says something similar: 'Then we ought not retaliate or render evil for evil to anyone, whatever evil we may have suffered from him.'[69]

Some have interpreted Jesus to mean that resorting to violence is always wrong no matter what the circumstances. Many early Christians understood Jesus' teaching that way and embraced non-violence even when they were being cruelly persecuted.

On the other hand, some believe there are biblical justifications for resorting to violence. The God of the Old Testament certainly seems to condone war. He commanded the Israelites to fight battles. God even picked their enemies and decided on when and how to eliminate them. On one occasion, he joined in the fight himself, throwing hailstones.[70] He even prevented the Sun from setting to give the Israelites more time to slaughter their foes.[71] God demanded the Israelites took no prisoners, insisting on the execution of men, women, and even children. The Old Testament God is a God of battle.

Most Christians believe God condones war in the right circumstances. When trying to determine when war is permitted, they often appeal to the thinking of the philosopher St Augustine. Augustine, who lived in the

Western Roman Empire, argued that Christians could in good conscience serve in the Roman military and engage in wars if two conditions were met. First, the war has to waged by a *legitimate authority*. In Augustine's day, that authority would have been the Emperor of the Western Roman Empire. The second condition is that there must be a *just cause*: a war should be fought to deal with a genuine injustice, and not just to, say, further the expansionist aims of those declaring war.

These two conditions were later augmented by other religious thinkers, including the twelfth-century philosopher St Thomas Aquinas. Aquinas adds that war should be fought with *good intention*. Aquinas realised that Augustine's first two conditions could be met by aggressors who, while they might happen to have justice on their side, were actually fighting for entirely bad and selfish reasons – perhaps just to capture more people and more land.

These three conditions have since been refined further still. The Spanish moralist Francisco de Vitoria (*c.* 1483–1546) adds the requirement that war should be fought properly. That's to say, force should not be used disproportionately, and innocent civilians should not be targeted. Nuking an entire civilian population in order to remedy some minor injustice is obviously unacceptable.

So, most of us – even most religious folk – maintain that individuals can sometimes justifiably resort to violence in self-defence or defence of the innocent. Most of us also suppose that states can justifiably wage war if certain conditions are met.

However, it's often controversial whether those conditions are in fact met. During World War II, the Allies bombed civilian populations. This looks like a pretty clear violation of Vitoria's requirement, but it was justified on the grounds that everyone was, in effect, a combatant because they were contributing in some way to the war effort.

According to some, the Iraq War of 2003 was fought for bad reasons. They argue that the war was being waged not by the relevant authority – the UN – but by the US and a few others going it alone. They also claim the war was fought for selfish reasons: to give the US strategic control over the Middle East and access to the enormous oil reserves located there. However, those arguing for war said the intention was to remove dangerous weapons of mass destruction and to free the people from a tyrannical regime. They also insisted that it was a war of last resort, all other methods for getting Saddam Hussein to disarm having been exhausted. People can usually find ways of applying the conditions for waging a just war to allow them either to support, or to oppose, any given war.

There have been some notable pacifist philosophers. Bertrand Russell defended what he called 'relative political pacifism'. He thought that going to war was *sometimes* justified, but that 'very few wars are worth fighting, and that the evils of war are almost always greater than they seem to excited populations at the moment when war breaks out'.[72] Russell called his pacifism 'relative' because he didn't place a blanket prohibition on going to war. He also called it 'political', because he thought we should expend our energy on finding ways of preventing our governments from engaging in unjustified wars – through acts of civil disobedience, for example. Russell was against British involvement in World War I. His protests against that war led to Russell being fined and his ability to travel restricted. Eventually he was imprisoned. Russell was also originally against going to war with Hitler, though eventually changed his mind.

Does a policy of *absolute* non-violence even make sense? The philosopher Jan Narveson argues that to say that violence is always morally wrong involves a contradiction. To say that violence is always wrong is to say that victims of violence have a right not to have violence inflicted on them. But such a right involves having the right to prevent violence being done to you, using violence if necessary. So, concludes Narveson, an absolute prohibition on violence gives us a right to use violence – it's a self-contradictory position.

In response to Narveson, philosopher Jonathan Glover points out that to say we have a right to protect ourselves from violence is not to say that we have a right to use any means necessary – including violence. As Glover says, 'To think that something is wrong is not to think its victims have a no-holds barred right of self-defence.'[73] So, absolute non-violence is not an incoherent position.

Still, absolute non-violence may not be a wise position to adopt. Some believe that a policy of non-violent resistance will ultimately always triumph. But will it? It's certainly true that non-violent resistance movements have been successful, and that in many situations it is an effective policy. Gandhi's non-violent protest at British rule did eventually succeed in removing the British from India. Martin Luther King's non-violent resistance to racial segregation also achieved its aim. However, while some non-violent movements have succeeded, others have failed. The non-violent resistance of the Tibetans to the 1950 invasion by China was met with brutal repression and appears entirely to have failed.

One obvious downside to adopting publicly a position of non-violence is that others then know that if they attack you, you won't retaliate with violence. Doesn't turning the other cheek just teach aggressors that aggression pays? So aren't we potentially increasing the risk of violence by embracing absolute non-violence? It's because of this concern, in particular, that many consider a policy of *absolute* non-violence unwise.

44. Have I found 'the one'?

> Result

Many of us are searching for 'the one' – our ideal
romantic partner. But is it a good idea to want to enter
into a lifelong romantic relationship with someone? While
many of us have a powerful desire for intimacy, friendship,
romance, and sex, and want these things as a package
in a relationship with just one person, not everyone thinks
that desire is entirely trustworthy.

The nineteenth-century philosopher Arthur
Schopenhauer notes that the feeling of romantic love is
extraordinarily potent, capable of driving people to do
foolish and dangerous things. It is an emotion so
intoxicating it can overwhelm us entirely. It can even lead
to suicide and murder. Yet the truth, says Schopenhauer,
is that the emotion is a trick played on us by nature.
Romantic love is an emotion nature has placed in us in
order to perpetuate our species. At root, the aim of all

this passion is sexual reproduction. We feel driven to seek out a romantic partner because we believe it will benefit us. However, the truth is it benefits only the perpetuation of the species. According to Schopenhauer: 'Nature attains her ends by implanting in the individual a certain illusion by which something which is in reality advantageous to the species alone seems to be advantageous to himself.'[74]

So, is our instinctive desire to find 'the one' a trick played on us by nature? Surely Schopenhauer is *too* cynical. Clearly, our desire for a romantic partner is in part a product of our evolutionary heritage. Its aim, from nature's perspective, is, at least in part, reproduction. Still, it's not that we don't also benefit as individuals from having a committed, supportive and loving life partner with whom to have children. Clearly, many of us do.

While Schopenhauer has a particularly cynical view of romantic love, others are hopelessly unrealistic and starry-eyed. Some believe that somewhere out there is the unique and perfect match for you, and the unique and perfect match for me. If and when we eventually find 'the one' with whom we are meant to be, they will complete us forever.

This view is nicely articulated in Plato's dialogue *Symposium*. Various men, including the philosopher Socrates and playwright Aristophanes, attend a drunken dinner party, giving speeches about love. Aristophanes tells a charming story about how all humans were once joined together as pairs. Some had two female halves, some had two male halves, and some had a male and a female half. Each of these peculiar creatures had four legs, four arms, four eyes and two mouths, and they got around by doing cartwheels. Unfortunately, these strange creatures tried to climb mount Olympus, planning to rebel against the gods. Zeus dealt with them by cutting each one of them into two. Each half now tries to find its other half, coupling with likely contenders. The pairs that were both female become coupled with other female halves – they are now lesbians. The pairs that were both males are now gay men. And the pairs that comprised male and female halves delight in coupling with members of the opposite sex. When someone does eventually find their *literal* other half, they want never to be separated again.

Lovely though Aristophanes' story is, it's pretty obviously false that each of us has a unique 'other half'. There's no single person specially made to complete you and only you. There are *many* people who could make you happy.

The person we end up with is to a large extent a matter of luck. It's down to factors such as which country we are born in, which places we live, our social class, and what university or social clubs we attend. Unless you believe in fate – that you are fated to be with a certain person located somewhere on the face of this planet, and that fate will somehow ensure you come together – it's pretty clear that who you end up with is largely a matter of luck. Had you been born in a different country, or born an aristocrat, or not attended that party on a particular day, then you would end up with a different life partner. And you'd be just as happy with that other partner – perhaps even happier.

So when we talk about finding 'the one', we don't usually mean finding *the one person in the whole world uniquely capable of completing us.* At least not if we're realists. Pretty obviously, and contrary to what Aristophanes suggests, that person does not exist. Rather, we just mean, say, identifying the person out of all those we have met or are likely to meet who would be the best fit for us. How do we know when we've found *that* person?

Choosing a life partner is certainly a balancing act. As we saw in 'Am I a perfectionist?', if you set the bar too high, you'll risk rejecting everyone as not good enough, and you'll end up with no one instead. Set the bar too low, on the other hand, and you may well live a life of regret, realising you settled for someone who's a poor fit for you.

It may be clichéd advice, but it's probably wise to look for someone who loves you for who you are. Avoid someone who sees you as a 'project' – as the raw material out of which they hope to forge their ideal partner. People aren't that malleable, and so they, and you, are likely to end up disappointed. And in any case, who wants to be someone else's creation?

Also avoid those who would prefer to clip your wings and frustrate your ambitions. Obviously, you should be looking for someone you love and who loves you. But it's also important to find someone who is supportive of you, who wants to help you achieve your goals, and delights in seeing you succeed. Supportive people empathise, listen to what you have to say, work with you as a team, and can be trusted to be there even when times get tough. If you find someone that ticks all these boxes, then you may indeed have found 'the one'.

45. Is there more to life than this?

Ask most people what reality is, and they'll probably point to the world we see around us and say: 'This is.' Reality is made up of dogs and houses, trees and mountains, stars and planets. We can't see *all* of reality, of course. We can't see the most distant galaxies or subatomic particles. But what we observe is at least *part of* reality as a whole. However, not all philosophers agree with this 'common sense' view. In particular, Plato doesn't agree. According to Plato, the real world is hidden. What we see around us are mere shadows or reflections of the real world.

Plato explains his view of reality with a story. At the bottom of the cave are prisoners chained to a wall. The prisoners can only see another wall before them. Behind them is a fire that casts shadows onto that wall. Objects are carried back and forth behind the prisoners, and the shadows cast by the objects appear on the wall. Because the prisoners can only see the wall, they take these shadows to be reality.

Then one prisoner is released. Initially, on turning round, the prisoner is blinded by the fire. But, once his eyes adjust, he recognises that what he had taken to be the real world was mere shadow play. The *real* objects had been hidden from sight. Then the prisoner is taken outside where he sees the Sun. Again, he is initially blinded. But, once his eyes adjust, he recognises that the Sun is the source of everything. When our newly-enlightened prisoner finally returns to the other captives, they refuse to believe his claim that they're being deceived and that reality is hidden from them. When he persists, they become irritated and attack him.

According to Plato, we're in a similar position to those prisoners. We are being fooled by our senses. We take what we see before us to be reality, but it's mere shadow play. In particular, the fleeting, changing things we observe before us – dogs and houses, trees and mountains – are mere shadows of the perfect, unchanging things hidden from our view.

How do we reveal this hidden reality? According to Plato, through the power of reason. True knowledge is knowledge of what Plato calls *the Forms* – the real things hidden from our senses. It can only be acquired through philosophical reasoning.

Of course, Plato's view that our senses can't provide us with knowledge of reality sounds odd to modern ears. We now believe that science – which is grounded in observation of the world – is the best, perhaps the only, way of finding out about reality. But if Plato is correct, if you want knowledge of reality, science is a waste of time.

Plato's views about reality have strongly influenced Christian thought. You can see an example of Plato's influence in the writings of C. S. Lewis, author of *The Lion, The Witch and The Wardrobe* and the other Narnia books. In *The Last Battle*, the final Narnia book, Narnia comes to an end. The land is covered by sea and the Sun is put out. All the good creatures from Narnia pass through a door into an amazing new place that is like the old Narnia, only far more wonderful. The children learn that the England and Narnia they had known were just shadows of the real world in which they now stand. Their teacher, Professor Digory Kirke, even explains: 'It's all in Plato, all in Plato: bless me, what do they teach them at these schools!' Finally, on the very last page, the children learn that they have died and passed over into this new place where they will live forever. Their old lives were just a dream; this is the morning of a new day. The 1993 film about C. S. Lewis is even called *Shadowlands*.

This talk of an extraordinary reality hidden from our gaze, a place to which we go when we die, is intoxicating stuff. It would be wonderful if it was true. But why should we believe it?

Plato provides several philosophical arguments for the existence of this extraordinary reality. The best-known argument is called the *One Over Many Argument*. It runs as follows.

Take a look at, say, five beautiful things: a beautiful vase, mountain, portrait, sunset, and flower. They all have *something in common*: they are all beautiful. So there's some *thing* that these, and all the other beautiful things, have in common – an *extra thing* that exists in addition to the many particular beautiful things. It's this extra thing – beauty – that makes them beautiful.

However, we don't observe this extra thing – beauty itself – in the world around us. For what we see is never *perfectly* beautiful. Even the most beautiful flower will have flaws. Also, what we observe is constantly changing. A beautiful flower lasts just a few days, and then decays. A beautiful sunset lasts but a few minutes. Beauty itself, however, will be perfectly beautiful and also unchanging. Plato calls this further thing – beauty itself – which is perfect and unchanging, the Form of beauty. Plato adds that the Form of beauty is that from which all the particular beautiful things we see around us derive their existence. They only exist because the Form does, much as shadows exist only because of the real things that cast them.

Plato argues that, just as there is a Form of beauty, so there must be a Form of the tree, and Form of the house, and Form of the cat – in fact, a Form for every kind of thing, living or inanimate. For, just as all beautiful things have something in common – beauty, so all trees have something in common – the Form of the tree. So there's an extra thing – the Form of the tree – that exists in addition to the particular trees we see. The Form is also perfect and unchanging, unlike the particular trees we see, which are always flawed, and eventually die.

So, Plato thinks there is a realm of perfect and unchanging Forms of which the particular dogs, houses, trees and mountains we see around us are mere fleeting shadows or reflections. These Forms are hidden from our senses.

Plato then adds a final Form by applying his One Over Many argument one more time. For of course the Forms are *themselves* a kind of thing: they're all Forms. So they too all have something in common. That extra *thing* is, then, *the Form of the Forms*.

The Form of the Forms is the ultimate Form, *the Form from which all existence and perfection ultimately flows*. Plato calls it the Form of the Good.

In Plato's analogy of the cave, the objects carried behind the prisoners are the Forms, and the Sun, which the prisoner recognises is the source of everything, is the Form of the Good.

This might all sound vaguely familiar. There's a perfect place we go when we die. There's an 'ultimately reality' from which all existence and perfection flows. That sounds a lot like heaven and God, doesn't it? Which is *not entirely coincidental.* Plato provides a view of ultimate reality that has been adopted by many religious thinkers down the ages, including C. S. Lewis. Our modern conception of God probably owes at least as much to philosophers like Plato as it does to the Old Testament.

When people ask, 'Is there more to life than this?' they often have in the back of their minds the thought that, like Plato's chained prisoners, we are taken in by an illusion. There's a higher reality on which we're missing out. The question is, *is that true*? It would be nice if were true that we go somewhere wonderful when we die. But has Plato given us good reason to believe it's true?

Plato himself was aware of problems with his One Over Many argument. One of the most famous difficulties with it is that it seems to *prove too much*. For example, if Plato's argument shows there is a Form of beauty, a Form of the tree, and a Form of the dog, then surely it also shows that there is a Form of poop – the 'something' all poops have in common. In fact, follow Plato's reasoning here and it seems there must be a Form for every disgusting, diseased, and cancerous thing. But now the realm of Forms doesn't sound quite so heavenly, does it? Who wants to go to heaven and be confronted by cosmic poop?

Conclusion: taking it further

If you have enjoyed this book, and would like to explore philosophy further, you might be interested in reading my books *The Philosophy Gym: 25 Short Adventures in Thinking* and *The Great Philosophers*. I can also highly recommend Nigel Warburton's *A Little History of Philosophy* as an introduction to the subject.

In addition to reading other books about philosophy, you might consider joining a philosophy club that meets up regularly, such as Philosophy in Pubs (see their website www.philosophyinpubs.co.uk for details) or critical thinking clubs such as the excellent Skeptics in the Pub (www.skepticsinthepub.org). Many other countries now have healthy philosophy and critical thinking discussion groups, with events taking place regularly. See, for example, Thinking While Drinking in the US, which has a website at http://thinkingwhiledrinking.org/. To find a suitable group near you, try searching 'philosophy' and critical thinking' on the Meetup website: www.meetup.com.

There are also some excellent, free philosophy MOOCs (Massive Open Online Courses) available online, as well as some fairly inexpensive accredited online courses on a range of topics available from, for example, the University of Oxford's Department for Continuing Education.

Notes

1 Quoted at
https://www.nytimes.com/2006/12/10/magazine/
10Section2b.t-7.html.
See also Jonathan R. Weaver and Jennifer K. Bosson, 'I Feel Like I Know You: Sharing Negative Attitudes of Others Promotes Feelings of Familiarity', in: *Personality and Social Psychology Bulletin*, Vol. 37, pp. 481–491. Published online 4 February 2011: https://journals.sagepub.com/doi/10.1177/0146167211398364

2 Aristotle, *Nichomachean Ethics*, Book VIII.

3 David Hume, *The Natural History of Religion*, §III.

4 Jiangang Liu, Jun Li, Lu Feng, Ling Li, Jie Tian, Kang Lee, 'Seeing Jesus in Toast: Neural and Behavioral Correlates of Face Pareidolia', in: *Cortex*, Vol. 53, April 2014, pp. 60–77.

5 Kathleen Taylor, 'Thought Crime', *Guardian*, 8 October 2005. Online: https://www.theguardian.com/world/2005/oct/08/terrorism.booksonhealth

6 2008 Ipsos/McClatchy poll: https://www.ipsos.com/en-us/news-polls/majority-americans-believe ghosts-57-and-ufos-52

7 Plato, 'Phaedo', in: *Introductory Readings in Ancient Greek and Roman Philosophy*, C.D.C. Reeve and Patrick Lee Miller, eds. (Indianapolis, IN: Hackett Publishing Co., 2006), 81b-d, p. 120.

8 'Belief in the paranormal and suggestion in the science room' by Richard Wiseman, Emma Greening, and Matthew Smith.

Br J Psychol. 2003 Aug;94 (Pt 3):285–97. Available online at: http://www.richardwiseman.com/resources/seanceBJP.pdf

9   John Locke, *Essay on Human Understanding*, Book III, Ch. XI. §6.

10 St Augustine, *The City of God*, Book XXI, Ch. 9.

11 'Middle Knowledge and Christian Exclusivism', on William Lane Craig's *Reasonable Faith* website: https://www. reasonablefaith.org/writings/scholarly-writings/christian-particularism/middle-knowledge-and-christian-exclusivism/

12 Anselm of Canterbury, *Cur Deus Homo*, Ch. 21.

13 Jonathan Edwards (1834), 'The End of the Wicked Contemplated by the Righteous: Or, the Torments of the Wicked in Hell, No Occasion of Grief to the Saints in Heaven', Sec. II.

14 Arthur Schopenhauer, 'On The Sufferings In The World'. First published 1851.

15 Ecclesiastes 4:2–3 (New International Version).

16 David Benatar, 'Kids? Just say No', in: *Aeon* magazine, online: https://aeon.co/essays/having-children-is-not-life-affirming-its-immoral

17 Epicurus, *Letter to Menoeceus*.

18 Aristotle, *Nicomachean Ethics*, Book I.

19 Immanuel Kant, 'Von den verschiedenen Rassen der Menschen' (1777)

20 Aristotle, *Politics*, Book1.

21 George Yancy, 'Dear White America' published in *The New York Times* in 2015. https://opinionator.blogs.nytimes.com/2015/12/24/dear-white-america/

22 *Ibid.*

23 David Broockman and Joshua Kalla, 'Supplementary Materials for Durably reducing transphobia: A field experiment on door-to-door canvassing', in: *Science*, Vol. 352, p. 220. Published 8

April 2016: http://science.sciencemag.org/content/sci/suppl/2016/04/07/352.6282.220.DC1/Broockman-SM.pdf

24 https://www.businessinsider.com/professionals-turn-to-psychics-in-uncertain-economy-2013–11?r=US&IR=T

25 'The Ethics of Belief', in: W. K. Clifford, *The Ethics of Belief and Other Essays* (Amherst, NY: Prometheus Books, 1999).

26 Harry Frankfurt, 'On Bullshit' (originally written in 1986, and published as a monograph in 2005).

27 Bertrand Russell, 'Fear, the Foundation of Religion', in his *Why I am Not a Christian, And Other Essays*, (New York: Touchstone, 1967), p. 22. First published in English in 1957.

28 See Richard Dawkins, 'Viruses of the Mind', in his *A Devil's Chaplain* (Boston: Houghton Mifflin, 2003).

29 There is a recent study by The Pew Research Center here: https://www.pewforum.org/2019/01/31/religions-relationship-to-happiness-civic-engagement-and-health-around-the-world/
A 2010 study suggests the increased happiness is a result of social networks built by attending religious services: 'Religion, Social Networks, and Life Satisfaction', by Chaeyoon Lim and Robert D. Putnam, American Sociological Review, 2010 75: 914.

30 Psychologist Professor Justin Barrett, who coined the acronym 'HADD', explains the hypothesis in detail in, for example, his *Why Would Anyone Believe in God?* (Walnut Creek, CA: AltaMira Press, 2004).

31 Galileo, *Il Saggiatore* ('The Assayer')

32 David Hume, *A Treatise of Human Nature*, Book III, Part I, Section I.

33 Survey by Ipsos Mori published in 2013: *Perils of Perception*. Available at: https://www.ipsos.com/ipsos-mori/en-uk/perceptions-are-not-reality

34 William James, *The Principles of Psychology*, 1890, Ch. 4.

35 *Ibid*.

36 Seneca, *On Anger*, Book III, 1.

37 Epictetus, *Discourses*, Book I, 1.

38 Seneca, *On Anger*, Book I, 11.

39 Seneca, *On Anger*, Book I, 8.

40 Marcus Aurelius, *Meditations*, 11.18.5.

41 Martha C. Nussbaum, 'Beyond Anger', in: *Aeon* magazine online: https://aeon.co/essays/there-s-no-emotion-we-ought-to-think-harder-about-than-anger

42 https://www.bbc.co.uk/news/43202075

43 *Ibid*.

44 https://ourworldindata.org/child-mortality

45 This quote appears in Robert Burton's 1621 *Anatomy of Melancholy*.

46 'Counting Blessings Versus Burdens: An Experimental Investigation of Gratitude and Subjective Well-Being in Daily Life', by Robert A. Emmons and Michael E. McCullough in *Journal of Personality and Social Psychology* 2003, Vol. 84, No. 2, 377–389.
Available here: https://greatergood.berkeley.edu/images/application_uploads/Emmons-CountingBlessings.pdf

47 Friedrich Nietzsche, 'Why I Am So Clever', in: *Ecce Homo*, Section 10. See, for example, *The Basic Writings of Nietzsche*, trans. and ed. by Walter Kaufmann (New York: Random House, 1967), p. 714.

48 https://howtobeaStoic.wordpress.com/2016/11/25/whats-the-point-of-regret/

49 Seneca, *On Anger*, Book III, 36.

50 See Peter Singer's book *The Life You Can Save: How To Play Your Part In Ending World Poverty* (New York: Random House, 2009).

51 'Genetic background of extreme violent behaviour', Tiihonen et al, Molecular Psychiatry volume 20, pages 786–792 (2015).

Notes

52 'The Psycho Gene', Philip Hunter, *EMBO Rep.* 2010 Sep; 11(9): 667–669.

53 See: https://www.princeton.edu/~joha/Johannes_Haushofer_CV_of_Failures.pdf

54 Paul McCartney to Sharyn Alfonsi on *CBS 60 Minutes.* https://www.forbes.com/sites/johnbaldoni/2018/12/12/paul-mccartney-keeping-it-real/#2f8d3e742132

55 *Scientific American* webpage: https://www.scientificamerican.com/article/why-success-breeds-success/

56 Quoted on Quora, September 2016, 156.

57 Hare, R. D. (2003). *The Hare Psychopathy Checklist—Revised* (2nd ed.). Toronto, ON, Canada: Multi-Health Systems.

58 Jonathan Glover, 'Into the Garden of Good and Evil', 158 *Guardian*, 13 October 1999.

59 Samuel P. Oliner and Pearl M. Oliner, *The Altruistic Personality – Rescuers of Jews in Nazi Europe* (New York: The Free Press, 1992), p. 179.

60 Quoted in 'The Hell of Our Choosing' by Edward Grippe in *Ethics and Phenomenology*, Mark Sanders and Jeremy Wisnewski (eds.), p. 118. See also the *No Exit* theatre playbill: https://sites.google.com/a/lclark.edu/clayton/commentaries/hell

61 Epictetus, *Discourses*, Book III.

62 Seneca, *Consolation to Helvia.*

63 Epictetus, *Discourses*, Book I.

64 Massimo Pigliucci, *How To Be A Stoic* (London: Rider Books, 2017), p. 190.

65 Mark Twain, *Captain Stormfield's Visit to Heaven.*

66 al-Ghazali, *Ihya Ulum-Id-Din*, Ch. 2.

67 Thomas Aquinas, *Summa Theologica*, I-II, qu. 64.

68 Matthew 5:39.

69 Plato, *Crito*, 49d.

70 Joshua 10:11.

71 Joshua 10:19.

72 Bertrand Russell, *Which Way to Peace*? (London: Michael Joseph, 1936), p.8.

73 Jonathan Glover, *Causing Death and Saving Lives* (London: Pelican, 1977), p. 257.

74 Arthur Schopenhauer 'Metaphysics of Love', available online at https://ebooks.adelaide.edu.au/s/schopenhauer/arthur/essays/chapter10.html)